Getting Started with React

A light but powerful way to build dynamic real-time
applications using ReactJS

Doel Sengupta

Manu Singhal

Danillo Corvalan

[PACKT] open source ✱
PUBLISHING   community experience distilled

BIRMINGHAM - MUMBAI

Getting Started with React

Copyright © 2016 Packt Publishing

First published: April 2016

Production reference: 1250416

Published by Packt Publishing Ltd.

Livery Place
35 Livery Street
Birmingham B3 2PB, UK.

ISBN 978-1-78355-057-9

www.packtpub.com

Credits

Authors
 Doel Sengupta

 Manu Singhal

 Danillo Corvalan

Reviewer
 Ilan Filonenko

Commissioning Editor
 Sarah Crofton

Acquisition Editor
 Rahul Nair

Content Development Editor
 Samantha Gonsalves

Technical Editor
 Mohit Hassija

Copy Editor
 Dipti Mankame

Project Coordinator
 Sanchita Mandal

Proofreader
 Safis Editing

Indexer
 Priya Sane

Graphics
 Kirk D'Penha

Production Coordinator
 Shantanu N. Zagade

Cover Work
 Shantanu N. Zagade

About the Authors

Doel Sengupta is a software programmer and is working in the industry for over 7 years, as a DevOps engineer and as a developer building enterprise level Web and mobile applications using RubyonRails and Rhomobile, Chef. Currently she is exploring the Javascript ecosystem. She has been a speaker in Ruby conferences. She finds interest in life sciences and has publications of her work in customised human joint prostheses design using Ansys & Mimics. She is an avid blogger (www.doels.net) writing about her technical and not-so-technical passions like culinary, photography, films. Follow her on twitter @doelsengupta.

Manu Singhal has been a programmer for 8 years and loves to code on Ruby and React. These days, he is busy cofounding a startup in e-commerce. In earlier roles, he has developed many enterprise and consumer based web/mobile applications and has also been a speaker at Ruby Conferences in India and the USA. He never misses a chance to play tennis and go hiking.

He has worked with Tata Consultancy Services and McKinsey & Company as a software developer and an architect.

He has contributed in books on Rhomobile and RubyMotion by Packt earlier.

Acknowledgments

We want to extend our heartfelt thanks to our family members and friends for their tireless support and belief. Our special thanks goes to Patrick Shaughnessy, Rohan Daxini and Kiprosh team, Abhishek Nalwaya, Akshat Paul, Naveen Rawat for taking out time to review the book. We also like to extend our gratitude to the ReactJS vibrant and ever enthusiastic online community, without which the vigorous task of writing such a book won't have been possible.

Thanks to the entire Packt publishing house especially Rahul Nair and team who helped in editing, proof reading and reviewing the book. As the famous saying goes "The journey is the reward", the very experience of writing this book is such a tremendous experience for us.

Danillo Corvalan is a software engineer who is passionate about software patterns and practices. He has a keen interest in the rapidly changing world of software development. He is quite insistent about the need of fast and reliable frameworks. He is originally from Brazil, now living in Amsterdam, the Netherlands. He loves biking a lot.

In Brazil, he worked on applications for the general public and lawyers, at the Court of Justice in his hometown city, Cuiabá/MT. Then, he moved to Florianópolis/SC, and worked at Bravi Software for developing hybrid and responsive web apps for education. Now, in Amsterdam, he is working at Vigour.io and helping to develop live multiscreen and responsive apps. From the web client-side perspective, in general, he has been in touch with technologies, such as vanilla JavaScript, jQuery, Backbone, and ReactJS.

For the past 5 years, Danillo has also worked with open source platforms and JavaScript on the server side (Node.js). He has played with React Native in order to develop native mobile applications with ReactJS.

About the Reviewers

Ilan is currently an undergraduate studying computer science in the College of Engineering at Cornell University. His interests in computer science stemmed from his early work in biophysics where he proposed a schematic that could potentially be used to synthetically create a proton transport Complex I and a virtual representation of the mitochondrion that can now function as the framework to synthesize a real biological system. Throughout his high school education and early years of college, he built various computational models and full-stack applications that showcased his expertise across a wide range of technologies from Mathematica to Ruby on Rails. In his first year of college, he cofounded and led the engineering team for four start-ups that have primarily disrupted their respective industries — MusicTech: Tunetap, MedTech: saund, FinTech: TheSimpleGroup, and FoodTech: Macrofuel. To this day, he contributes to these ventures as a project manager and continues to lead the backend engineering initiative for two Cornell engineering project teams. In addition to his academics and entrepreneurial endeavors, he works as a part-time software engineer for the R&D division at Bloomberg L.P., where he spent two summers researching and optimizing their distributed systems platform for large-scale data analytics.

www.PacktPub.com

eBooks, discount offers, and more

Did you know that Packt offers eBook versions of every book published, with PDF and ePub files available? You can upgrade to the eBook version at www.PacktPub.com and as a print book customer, you are entitled to a discount on the eBook copy. Get in touch with us at customercare@packtpub.com for more details.

At www.PacktPub.com, you can also read a collection of free technical articles, sign up for a range of free newsletters and receive exclusive discounts and offers on Packt books and eBooks.

https://www2.packtpub.com/books/subscription/packtlib

Do you need instant solutions to your IT questions? PacktLib is Packt's online digital book library. Here, you can search, access, and read Packt's entire library of books.

Why subscribe?

- Fully searchable across every book published by Packt
- Copy and paste, print, and bookmark content
- On demand and accessible via a web browser

Table of Contents

Preface

Learning ReactJS is a light but powerful way to build fantastic UI components! This book will help you develop robust, reusable, and fast user interfaces with ReactJS. This book will ensure a smooth and seamless transition to the ReactJS ecosystem. The books is full of hands on real applications. From setup to implementation, testing, and deployment: discover the new frontier of front-end web development. ReactJS, popularly known as V of MVC architecture, is developed by the Facebook and Instagram developers. We will take a deep dive on the ReactJS world and explore the unidirectional data flow, virtual DOM, DOM difference, which ReactJS leverages in order to increase the performance of the UI. You will learn the key concepts of ReactJS in a step-by-step process. You will also learn ES6 syntaxes used in ReactJS for the future browsers, with the transpiling techniques to be used in order to support it in current browsers.

You will not only learn to apply and implement ReactJS concepts but also know how you can test JS-based applications and deploy them. In addition to this, you will also be developing a full-fledged application using Flux architecture. You will also learn about Redux, which lets you understand how you can manipulate the data in ReactJS applications easily, by introducing some limitations on the updates. With ample codes covering the concepts and their theoretical explanations coupled with screenshots of the application, you will gain a deep understanding of ReactJS.

What this book covers

Chapter 1, Getting Started with ReactJS, is a brief overview of React about where to download and how to make it work on your web page. It will demonstrate how to create your first React component.

Chapter 2, Exploring JSX and the ReactJS Anatomy, will show the same simple react component, created in the first chapter, built with the JSX syntax. It'll explain the purpose of JSX and demystify its usage. It will compare some older template techniques to JSX and try to clarify some common questions about it.

Chapter 3, Working with Properties, will make you start developing your own app. It will use Facebook Open Graph API. This will cover how to configure it, get your friends' list, and render it using React. After this, we're going to break UI into small components.

Chapter 4, Stateful Components and Events, covers components that have state, practices to communicate between them, and how to respond to 'users' input/events in order to have UI reflect this state. This chapter also covers how the state changes your React UI performance with the Virtual DOM.

Chapter 5, Component Life cycle and Newer ECMAScript in React, explores what is the life cycle of such a React component. Furthermore, we will also dig into the future ECMA Script syntaxes and few changes that the React community also used from version 0.13.0. For this, we will review some ES6 and ES7 features within the react library.

Chapter 6, Reacting with Flux, will explain the flux architecture, which is used to build client-side web applications. It complements React's composable view components by using a unidirectional data flow. There is an in-depth explanation of all the components of the FLUX architecture (view, stores, action, and dispatchers).

Chapter 7, Making Your Component Reusable, will cover React good practices and patterns. This includes practices to develop reusable components, how to structure your components hierarchically to a better data flow and how to validate your components behavior.

Chapter 8, Testing React components, will show how to test your React code as this has never been so easy in React. To do so, we're going to unit test our app developed so far.

Chapter 9, Preparing Your Code for Deployment, tells us that React comes with a transformer for JSX that works on the fly. This should never be deployed in production though. This chapter will talk you through the ways of building those files offline using node libs, such as Webpack and Gulp.

Chapter 10, What's Next, explains some other advanced concepts, such as react-router, react-ajax, hot-reloading, redux, isomorphic apps, and so on.

What you need for this book

The basic requirement is NodeJS followed by the installation of npm packages, like react, react-tools, express etc. Complete list chapter-wise is given below:

Chapter number	Software required (With version)
1	Nodejs 4.2.4 ReactJS: • `http://fb.me/react-0.14.7.js` (development) • `http://fb.me/react-0.14.7.min.js` (production) JSXTransformer : • `https://cdnjs.cloudflare.com/ajax/libs/react/0.13.3/JSXTransformer.js` Install Python or httpster for serving webserver Chrome / Mozilla ReactJS addon/extension for browser JS tool
2	npm install react-tools
3	Open-Graph JavaScript SDK: `https://developers.facebook.com/docs/javascript`
5	ReactJS version 0.13.0 or above JSXTransformer (0.13.3)
8	Npm install -g -d chai mocha jest-cli babel-loader babel-preset-es2015 babel-preset-react babel-preset-stage-2 react-addons-test-utils
9	npm install -g webpack browserify npm install --save-dev gulp gulp-concat gulp-uglify gulp-react gulp-html-replace npm install --save-dev vinyl-source-stream browserify watchify reactify gulp-streamify
10	npm instal express npm install react-redux

Who this book is for

Whether you are new to the JS world or an experienced JS developer, this book will ensure to glide you seamlessly in the ReactJS ecosystem. You will not only know and implement the ReactJS concepts but also learn how can you test JS-based applications and deploy them. In addition to these, you will also be introduced to Flux and build applications based on Flux Application Architecture, which is not a full-fledged framework but an architecture. You will also learn about Redux, which lets you understand how you can easily manipulate the data in ReactJS applications, by introducing some limitations on the updates. With ample codes covering the concepts explained theoretically and screenshots of the application, you will have a simple yet deep understanding of ReactJS.

Conventions

In this book, you will find a number of text styles that distinguish between different kinds of information. Here are some examples of these styles and an explanation of their meaning.

Code words in text, database table names, folder names, filenames, file extensions, pathnames, dummy URLs, user input, and Twitter handles are shown as follows: "Once Sublime editor is installed, go to the installed directory, and you can open Sublime from the terminal by running `subl` in the directory that your are in and you will open the files of the current directory in sublime."

A block of code is set as follows:

```
<!DOCTYPE html>
<html>
<head>
  <script src="fb-react-0.12.2.js"></script>
</head>
<body>
  <div id="root"></div>
</body>
</html>
```

When we wish to draw your attention to a particular part of a code block, the relevant lines or items are set in bold:

```
function loadUserAndLikes () {
  FB.api('/me', function (userResponse) {
    React.render(<UserDetails userDetails={userResponse} />,
    document.getElementById('user'));
```

```
    var fields = { fields: 'category,name,picture.type(normal)'
    };
    FB.api('/me/likes', fields, function (likesResponse) {
      React.render(<UserLikesList list={likesResponse.data} />,
      document.getElementById('main'));
    });
  });
}
```

Any command-line input or output is written as follows:

```
sudo npm install jest-cli -save-dev
```

New terms and **important words** are shown in bold. Words that you see on the screen, for example, in menus or dialog boxes, appear in the text like this: " I've experienced using Atom on a MacOS X Yosemite is that the font quality looks poorer than that in Sublime Text. If you face it, you just need to uncheck the **Use Hardware Acceleration** option in Atom's settings.."

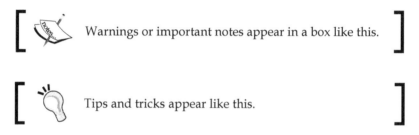

Warnings or important notes appear in a box like this.

Tips and tricks appear like this.

Reader feedback

Feedback from our readers is always welcome. Let us know what you think about this book—what you liked or disliked. Reader feedback is important for us as it helps us develop titles that you will really get the most out of.

To send us general feedback, simply e-mail feedback@packtpub.com, and mention the book's title in the subject of your message.

If there is a topic that you have expertise in and you are interested in either writing or contributing to a book, see our author guide at www.packtpub.com/authors.

Customer support

Now that you are the proud owner of a Packt book, we have a number of things to help you to get the most from your purchase.

Downloading the example code

You can download the example code files for this book from your account at http://www.packtpub.com. If you purchased this book elsewhere, you can visit http://www.packtpub.com/support and register to have the files e-mailed directly to you.

You can download the code files by following these steps:

1. Log in or register to our website using your e-mail address and password.
2. Hover the mouse pointer on the **SUPPORT** tab at the top.
3. Click on **Code Downloads & Errata**.
4. Enter the name of the book in the **Search** box.
5. Select the book for which you're looking to download the code files.
6. Choose from the drop-down menu where you purchased this book from.
7. Click on **Code Download**.

Once the file is downloaded, please make sure that you unzip or extract the folder using the latest version of:

- WinRAR / 7-Zip for Windows
- Zipeg / iZip / UnRarX for Mac
- 7-Zip / PeaZip for Linux

Downloading the color images of this book

We also provide you with a PDF file that has color images of the screenshots/ diagrams used in this book. The color images will help you better understand the changes in the output. You can download this file from http://www.packtpub.com/ sites/default/files/downloads/Bookname_ColorImages.pdf.

Errata

Although we have taken every care to ensure the accuracy of our content, mistakes do happen. If you find a mistake in one of our books — maybe a mistake in the text or the code — we would be grateful if you could report this to us. By doing so, you can save other readers from frustration and help us improve subsequent versions of this book. If you find any errata, please report them by visiting `http://www.packtpub.com/submit-errata`, selecting your book, clicking on the **Errata Submission Form** link, and entering the details of your errata. Once your errata are verified, your submission will be accepted and the errata will be uploaded to our website or added to any list of existing errata under the Errata section of that title.

To view the previously submitted errata, go to `https://www.packtpub.com/books/content/support` and enter the name of the book in the search field. The required information will appear under the **Errata** section.

Piracy

Piracy of copyrighted material on the Internet is an ongoing problem across all media. At Packt, we take the protection of our copyright and licenses very seriously. If you come across any illegal copies of our works in any form on the Internet, please provide us with the location address or website name immediately so that we can pursue a remedy.

Please contact us at `copyright@packtpub.com` with a link to the suspected pirated material.

We appreciate your help in protecting our authors and our ability to bring you valuable content.

Questions

If you have a problem with any aspect of this book, you can contact us at `questions@packtpub.com`, and we will do our best to address the problem.

1
Getting Started with ReactJS

In this chapter, we are going to look at an overview of ReactJS—what it is and some highlights on what this powerful and flexible library does. We'll also learn how to download and make it work in a small application. In this chapter, we will cover the following topics:

- Introducing ReactJS
- Downloading ReactJS
- Tools
- Trying ReactJS

Introducing ReactJS

ReactJS is a JavaScript library, created by Facebook and Instagram, in order to build user interfaces (UIs) that can respond to users' input events along with creating and maintaining states. States are used to maintain changes to components, which will be covered in detail in later chapters. The page loads faster by comparing only the changed and the updated part of the web page (we will cover Virtual **DOM** (**Document Object Model**) in more detail in *Chapter 4, Stateful Components and Events*). React provides a one-way data flow that reduces complexity compared with a traditional data-binding system, which facilitates creating reusable and encapsulated components. We will also explore React data flow in *Stateful Components and Events* chapter and how to make your UI components more reusable in *Chapter 7, Making Your Components Reusable*.

ReactJS is not just another JavaScript library though many developers consider it to be the V of the MVC application. It drives you through building reusable components, rethinking your UI and best practices. Nowadays, performance and portability are vital to build user interfaces, mainly due to the large use of Internet-accessible devices and the fast-paced developmental phases of the projects. This can result in complex frontend code. The need for using a library that helps your code to grow in both performance and quality is really important; otherwise, you just end up writing big HTML files with UI logic everywhere that takes ages to modify and can compromise code quality. ReactJS encourages the best practices shown here:

- Following a pattern
- Separating concerns
- Splitting your UI into components
- Communication between components with one-way data flow
- Use of properties and states appropriately

ReactJS is a library that takes care of the UI (Views) differently from a framework. Let's say we are building a **Single Page Application** (**SPA**) and we want to handle a routing system, we can use whatever library we want that deals with routing. This applies to every other part of the technology stack required to build a SPA except the UI or, as some say, the View, when working on an MVC/MV* architecture. In the ReactJS world, when you're talking about the view, actually you're talking about a component. They are a little different from each other. A React component holds both logic and behavior of the View. In general, a single component represents a small part of the View, whereas many of these components together represent the whole View of the application.

We will be discussing more about MVC/MV* and FLUX architecture in *Chapter 6, Reacting with FLUX*.

 MVC stands for Model View Controller and MV* for Model View Whatever.

It is very straightforward to build or change just a small part of your web application. Facebook did that with their commenting interface. They replaced it with one made in ReactJS. There is detailed code at https://facebook.github.io/react/docs/tutorial.html about how the comments appear in Facebook using ReactJS.

This commenting interface, which the Facebook development team explained, gives us the live updates and *Optimistic commenting*, in which the comments are shown in the list before having been saved on the server. There is also a Facebook developer plugin, which enables users to add comments in your website using their Facebook accounts (`https://developers.facebook.com/docs/plugins/comments`).

One of my experiences was to build a survey app in ReactJS and place it in some web application already in production. ReactJS provides a bunch of life cycle events, which facilitates the integration with other libraries, plugins, and even frameworks. In *Chapter 5*, *Component Life Cycle*, we will go through all the life cycle phases of a React component, and in *Chapter 7*, *Making Your Component Reusable*, we will be incorporating validations and organizing our code using Mixins.

ReactJS understands the UI elements as objects. When building React components, we will modularize the code by encapsulating the view logic and the view representation. This is another feature that supports componentization and is one of the reasons for Virtual DOM to work. React code can also be written in another syntax, JSX (an extension to ECMASCRIPT), instead of JavaScript. Although it is not mandatory to use, it is easy to use and increases the readability of the code. We're going to dig more into JSX and see how it works and why it's necessary in *Chapter 2*, *Exploring JSX*.

Who uses ReactJS?

ReactJS is one of the emerging JavaScript libraries to build web UI components, and some big companies are already using it in production. They are as follows:

- The Instagram website
- Facebook comments, page insights, business management tools, Netflix, Yahoo, Atlassian, and most new JS development
- New JS development for Khan Academy, PayPal, AirBnb, Discovery Digital Networks, and many more
- Some projects inside *The New York Times*

Downloading ReactJS

Before we start coding some ReactJS, we need to download it. You can download ReactJS through their website, `http://facebook.github.io/react/downloads.html`.

At the time of writing this book, ReactJS is currently at version 0.14.7. Two versions of ReactJS scripts are provided—one is for development, which has all the core code with comments if you want to debug or even contribute to them. The other one is for production, which includes extra performance optimizations. Here are the links of the versions of the script for downloading:

- `http://fb.me/react-0.14.7.js` (development)
- `http://fb.me/react-0.14.7.min.js` (production)

Versions of 0.13.0 and higher contain a huge set of enhancements. There is a support for the ES6 class syntax and removal of mix-ins, which are covered in *Chapter 5, Component Life Cycle and Newer ECMAscript in ReactJS*.

Inside the ReactJS downloads page, there are other versions of the ReactJS script with add-ons. This script extends the ReactJS library to support animations and transitions, and also provides some other utilities that are not part of core React. There is no need to download this version for now because we're not going to use those features in the following examples.

There is also the JSX transformer script for download. You can download it at `https://cdnjs.cloudflare.com/ajax/libs/react/0.13.3/JSXTransformer.js`.

It should only be used in the development environment and not in production. JSX will be covered in more detail in the *Chapter 2, Exploring JSX and the ReactJS Anatomy*.

If you are using a tool to control your dependencies, such as **Node Package Manager (NPM)** or **Bower**, it's also possible to download ReactJS through these tools. Details can be found at `https://facebook.github.io/react/downloads.html`.

Installing ReactJS with NPM

Check whether `node` is already installed on your machine using `node -v`.

Otherwise, install the node packages from their website (`https://nodejs.org/en/`), based on your operating system.

We cover installing packages through NPM in *Chapter 8, Testing React Components* and *Chapter 9, Deployment*.

If you have `Node` and NPM configured on your machine, execute the following command inside your application's folder from any console tool to install `react-tools`:

```
npm install react-tools
```

Once installed, you can reference React dependency as follows:

```
Var React = require('react');
```

From now on, you can use the `React` variable and its methods, such as `React.createClass({...});`. Remember that because you've installed it using NPM, it's required that you bundle your code or transform it to a static asset before testing your application. In *Chapter 2*, *Exploring JSX*, we're going to cover some transform tools that you might use. You can check for more details about deployment in *Chapter 8*, *Preparing Your Code for Deployment*.

Installing ReactJS with Bower

Unlike NPM, Bower controls browser-ready packages, so it's also the same. Apart from using the NPM packages, we can also use Bower-ready packages (`https://facebook.github.io/react/downloads.html`). Bower helps to maintain all the packages by installing and maintaining the correct versions of the necessary packages (`http://bower.io/`).

First, make sure that you have Bower installed and configured. After this, execute the following command:

```
bower install --save react
```

This will save ReactJS as a dependency in you Bower configuration file. Now you just need to reference that in your HTML code. By default, it's provided at `./bower_components/react/react.js`. The minified version is also provided in the same folder at `react.min.js`.

Tools

The community has already developed a bunch of tools to improve our coding experience and productivity. In this section, we'll get through some text editors, their packages, and a browser extension created to improve debugging applications in ReactJS.

Text editors

Most of the text editors available today provide syntax highlighting for JSX and useful snippets and helpers for ReactJS. Here are some text editors that I suggest using:

- Vim — `http://www.vim.org/download.php`
- Emacs Editor — `https://www.gnu.org/software/emacs/`
- Sublime Text — `http://www.sublimetext.com/`
- Atom — `https://atom.io/`
- Brackets — `http://brackets.io/`

Sublime Text requires a paid license although it works in free mode, always showing a popup that might trouble you from time to time. Also, you will need to install its package manager separately. You can find sublime Text packages and more information on how to install its package manager at `https://packagecontrol.io/`. Once the Sublime editor is installed, go to the installed directory, and you can open Sublime from the terminal by running `subl` in the directory that your are in and you will open the files of the current directory in Sublime.

Atom is recent and free and was made by GitHub. It comes with a package manager included and there is no need to install it separately. You just need to go to the settings and install the React package. It comes with syntax highlights, snippets, and so on. The only problem I've experienced using Atom on a MacOS X Yosemite is that the font quality looks poorer than that in Sublime Text. If you face it, you just need to uncheck the **Use Hardware Acceleration** option in Atom's settings.

Brackets is also free and has a lot of great features such as live preview; for example, you can edit your code files and see the changes being applied in the browser. Brackets has a built-in extension manager, and you can install ReactJS JSX syntax highlighting as well. However, at the time of writing this book, some highlighting features were not working well.

All of these text editors are pretty good and have lots of features, but it's not the purpose of this book to show them. Feel free to choose one if you don't have a preferred text editor already.

Chrome extension

The ReactJS team created a browser extension for Google Chrome. It allows you to inspect the component hierarchy, and it helps a lot when you need to debug your application. You can open **Chrome Web Store**, search for **React Developer Tools**, and install it. You need to open **Chrome Developer Tools** (*F12* on Windows and Linux, *⌘-Option-I* on Mac) to use the extension. We're going to use the extension in later chapters to understand the ReactJS component hierarchy. In order to have the React extension/add-on work in Chrome/Firefox, we need to have a React component globally available on the web page.

Trying ReactJS

It is time to hack some code and create our first application with ReactJS. We'll start configuring React in a simple web page by adding the ReactJS script dependency. Then, we'll create a JavaScript file that will hold our ReactJS component code and render it in an HTML element.

Then, we'll rebuild the same example using JSX syntax and learn how to configure that in the page. Don't worry about JSX for now as it will be covered in detail in the *Chapter 2, Exploring JSX and the ReactJS Anatomy.*

This is going to be a simple application for learning purposes. In following chapters, we're going to create a full web application that will consume the Facebook Open Graph API, log in with your Facebook's account, render your friend list, and so on. So, let's get our hands dirty!

Configuring ReactJS in a web page

After downloading ReactJS scripts dependencies, we need to create an HTML file with a simple element inside its body. We're going to call the file `root.html`. It will be responsible for rendering our ReactJS component.

Here is how your HTML file should look like:

```
<!DOCTYPE html>
<html>
<head>
  <script src="http://fb.me/react-0.12.2.js"></script>
</head>
<body>
  <div id="root"></div>
</body>
</html>
```

It references Facebook CDN scripts, but you can reference the scripts that we have downloaded (fb-react-0.12.2.js) locally.

Here is how your HTML file should look like if the locally downloaded ReactJS file is used instead of CDN:

```
<!DOCTYPE html>
<html>
<head>
  <script src="fb-react-0.12.2.js"></script>
</head>
<body>
  <div id="root"></div>
</body>
</html>
```

Creating your first React component

Now create a JavaScript file named hello-world.js and reference that in the HTML file by placing this code after the root div element:

```
<div id="root"></div>
<script src="hello-world.js"></script>
```

We will make use of React.createElement to create React element. The format of React.createElement is:

```
ReactElement createElement(
  string/ReactClass type,
  [object props],
  [children ...]
)
```

Paste the following code into hello-world.js:

```
var HelloWorld = React.createClass({
  render: function () {
    return React.createElement('h1', null, "Hello World from
    Learning ReactJS");

  }
});

React.render(
  React.createElement(HelloWorld, null),
```

```
    document.getElementById('root')
);

In the above code
return React.createElement('h1', null, "Hello World from Learning
ReactJS");
h1 → Is the type of HTML element to be created
null → means there is no object properties presentation
Third argument → the content of the h1 tag
```

Details of this code will be covered in more detail in the following chapters.

Now open the page in any browser and check that it created an h1 html element and placed the text inside it. You should see something like this:

Configuring JSX

Now we are going to make the same application using JSX syntax. First, we need to configure that in our HTML page by adding the JSX transformer script file JSXTransformer-0.12.2.js after the ReactJS script react-0.12.2.js within the head element:

```
<head>
  <script src="http://fb.me/react-0.12.2.js"></script>
  <script src="http://fb.me/JSXTransformer-0.12.2.js"></script>
</head>
```

You also need to change the hello-world.js type reference to text/jsx in the HTML page. It must be like this:

```
<script type="text/jsx" src="hello-world.js"></script>
```

Serving files through the web server

Google Chrome doesn't accept requests to local files of type text/jsx, it throws a cross-origin request error (commonly named as the CORS error). CORS is sharing a resource on a different domain than the current one. Chrome security doesn't allow it by default; however, you can access it on Firefox and Safari. It's also possible to work around with CORS errors by starting a local server, such as Python, Node, or any other web server you want.

Another way is to install the node package httpster:

```
npm install -g httpster
```

Once installed, run the command httpster from the react application directory. The application will load up in your browser (default port 3333):

```
doel@doel-Vostro-3500:~/reactjs/ch10/app1$ httpster
Starting HTTPster v1.0.1 on port 3333 from /home/doel/reactjs/ch10/app1
```

Another way is to install the simple Python server. Install it and run its command inside the folder you want to serve and then you're ready to go. You can find out how to install python at https://www.python.org/. After installing python, you can run the following command inside your project folder:

```
python -m SimpleHTTPServer
```

It will output a message saying the port it's running such as Serving HTTP on 0.0.0.0 port 8000. You can now navigate to http://localhost:8000/. If this port is being used by another application, consider passing the desired port number as the last parameter in the same command as follows:

```
python -m SimpleHTTPServer 8080
```

If you don't want to use python, ReactJS has provided a tutorial page with scripts in other languages to run a simple web server and you should be able to test it. You can check it out at https://github.com/reactjs/react-tutorial/.

Creating a React component with the JSX syntax

With our HTML page configured, we can now change the `hello-world.js` script file to follow the JSX Syntax. Your script file should look like this:

```
var HelloWorld = React.createClass({
  render: function () {
    return <h1>Hello World from Learning ReactJS</h1>;
  }
});

React.render(
  <HelloWorld />,
  document.getElementById('root')
);
```

It will generate the same result as in the previous `Hello World` example. As you can see, there is no need to call the `createElement` method explicitly.

Thus, the JSX will produce the same output as the JavaScript, but without the extra braces and semicolons.

In the following chapter, *Chapter 2, Exploring JSX and the ReactJS Anatomy* you're going to learn how JSX works and why it is highly recommended.

Summary

In this chapter, you learned what ReactJS is, downloaded it, and used it in a small application. We have created our first React component and reviewed key benefits of this powerful library.

In the next chapter, we are going to dive into JSX and learn how to build some practical components that demonstrate this powerful extension syntax. We'll also learn some "gotchas" and best practices and learn why JSX suits our needs when developing a React components presentation.

2
Exploring JSX and the ReactJS Anatomy

In this chapter, you are going to explore the JSX syntax and learn what it is and why it makes it easier for us to understand UI components. You will learn about the ReactJS anatomy and code some common scenarios in order to demonstrate this efficient syntax so that we can step forward in next chapters and build a full application. This chapter will walk you through the following topics:

- What is JSX?
- The ReactJS anatomy
- JSX Gotchas

What is JSX?

JSX is a JavaScript syntax extension that looks similar to XML. It is used to build UI components in ReactJS. It's very similar to HTML with some subtle differences. JSX extends JavaScript in such a way that you can easily build ReactJS components with the same understanding as building HTML pages. It's commonly mixed with your JavaScript code because ReactJS thinks about UI in a different way. This paradigm will be explained later in the chapter.

It's wrong to say that you are mixing up your HTML with JavaScript. As already said, JSX extends JavaScript. Actually, you're not writing HTML tags, but you're writing JavaScript objects in the JSX syntax. Of course, it has to be transformed into plain JavaScript first.

When you write this example:

```
var HelloWorld = React.createClass({
  render: function () {
    return <h1>Hello World from Learning ReactJS</h1>;
  }
});
```

It's transformed into this:

```
var HelloWorld = React.createClass({
  render: function () {
    return React.createElement('h1', null, "Hello World from
    Learning ReactJS");   }
});
```

This transformer script file detects JSX notations and transforms them into plain JavaScript notations. These scripts and tools should never be placed in a production environment because it would be painful for the server to transform the script on every request. For the production environment, we should provide the transformed file. We will be covering that process later in this chapter.

As discussed in *Chapter 1, Getting Started with ReactJS*, note the following:

- `ReactElement` is the primary API of React. ReactElement has four properties: `type`, `props`, `key`, and `ref`.

- ReactElement has no methods of itself, and nothing has been defined on the prototype also.

- ReactElement objects can be created by calling the `React.createElement` method.

- In the highlighted code mentioned earlier, we can see that the first argument for the `React.createElement` method is creating an `h1` element, with properties being passed as null and the actual content of the `h1` element being the string `Hello World from Learning ReactJS`

- ReactElements are passed into DOM in order to create a new tree in DOM.

- ReactElements are named virtual DOM and are not the same as DOM elements. Details of virtual DOM will be discussed in later chapters.

- As per the official React documentation (`https://facebook.github.io/react/docs/glossary.html`), "ReactElement is a light, stateless, immutable, virtual representation of a DOM Element".

Let's check our previous example again when we didn't use the JSX syntax:

```
React.createElement('h1', null, "Hello World from Learning
ReactJS");
```

This code is creating an `h1` element. Think about it being like creating an element through JavaScript with the `document.createElement()` function, which makes the code very readable.

JSX is not mandatory, but it's highly recommended. It is painful to create large and complex components using JavaScript. For example, if we want to create nested elements using JSX, we would need to do the following:

```
var CommentList = React.createClass({
  render: function() {
    return (
        <ul>
            <li>ReactJS</li>
            <li>JSX</li>
            <li>
                <input type="text" />
                <button>Add</button>
            </li>
        </ul>
    );
  }
});
```

However, using plain JavaScript ReactJS objects, it would look like this:

```
var CommentList = React.createClass({displayName: "CommentList",
  render: function() {
    return (
        React.createElement("ul", null,
            React.createElement("li", null, "ReactJS"),
            React.createElement("li", null, "JSX"),
            React.createElement("li", null,
                React.createElement("input", {type: "text"}),
                React.createElement("button", null, "Add")
            )
        )
    );
  }
});
```

We can see a big scary component that might grow in case of more complex logic. Such complex components are difficult to maintain and understand.

Why JSX?

In general, HTML and JavaScript are segregated in frameworks by defining UI or a view to represent their mutable data, which normally is a template language and/or a display logic interpreter. The following is some jQuery code:

```html
<html>
  <head>
    <title>Just an example</title>
  </head>
  <body>
    <div id="my-awesome-app">
      <!-- Here go my rendered template -->
    </div>

    <script id="my-list" type="text/html">
      <ul>
        {{each items}}
          <li>
            ${name}
          </li>
        {{/each}}
      </ul>
    </script>
  </body>
</html>
```

The `script` element represents a template component that will be rendered in the `my-awesome-app` div element. The code here is a JavaScript file that pushes data to that template and asks jQuery to do the job and render the UI:

```
$("#my-list").tmpl(serverData).appendTo("#my-my-awesome-app");
```

Whenever you want to put some display logic on that code, you will need to rely on both JavaScript and HTML files. In other words, a single component is a mix of files—normally, a JavaScript file that controls the view, a template/markup file representing the view, and a model/service that fetches data from the server and sends it to the view. Typically in an MVC application, the logic of M(model), V(view), and C(controller) are separated in order to provide the separation of concern and better readability and maintenance of the code.

Let's say that we now have to change this view and need to hide the list when the user is not logged in. Considering that the model/service code is already bringing this information, we'll have to change both the code that controls the view and the markup one in order to apply those changes. Harder the change is, more painful it is to apply those changes. Our code ends up in big JavaScript and HTML files, mixed up with display logic, template expressions, and business code.

Although you are an experienced frontend developer, apply some separation of concerns, and split your UI into smaller views, you end up with hundreds of files just to represent a single piece of UI: view controller, HTML template, style sheet, and your model. It makes a small application look complex with that amount of files, and you'll certainly get messy wondering which file is part of a specific view or component.

The thing we want to show here is that we've been mixing markup and logic code since the beginning, but other than that, we've also been splitting them into other files, making it more difficult to find and to modify them.

ReactJS with JSX drives you in the other way. There is a really interesting paragraph in the ReactJS official page that honestly reasons this powerful library and its paradigm:

> *"We strongly believe that components are the right way to separate concerns rather than "templates" and "display logic." We think that markup and the code that generates it are intimately tied together. Additionally, display logic is often very complex and using template languages to express it becomes cumbersome.* (http://facebook.github.io/react/docs/displaying-data. html#jsx-syntax)

We like to think of ReactJS components as a single source of truth. All other locations that use your component will be just references. Every change you apply to the original one will be propagated to all other places referencing it. Customization is easily done through properties and child componentization. JSX is like a middleware that converts your markup code to objects where ReactJS can handle them.

JSX speeds up the frontend development in ReactJS. Instead of creating literal objects to represent your UI, you create XML-like elements very similar to HTML, and you can even reference other components that you've created. Also, it's very straightforward to reuse third-party components or even publish your own. In a corporate environment, you could have a commonly used components repository that other projects can import from.

Tools for transforming JSX

The JSX Transformer file and other tools, as already mentioned, are responsible for transforming your JSX syntax into plain JavaScript. The ReactJS team and the community provide some tools for that. Such tools can deal with any kind of file since they have JavaScript code and JSX syntax. In older versions of React, a comment was required on the first line of `.js` files such as `/** @jsx React.DOM */`. Thankfully, this was removed after version 0.12.

JSX Transformer has been deprecated now. Instead, we can use `https://babeljs.io/repl/` to compile the JSX syntax into JavaScript. To include JSX in your script tag, either use `<script type="text/jsx">` or while transforming, use `babel`

```
<script type="text/babel">.
```

Earlier there was an online tool at `http://facebook.github.io/react/jsx-compiler.html`. However, the React developer team discontinued it, and JSX Transformer has been deprecated.

Since such JSX transformation would take a substantial computation at the client side, we should *not* be doing these transformations in production environments. Instead, we should use:

```
npm install -g babel-cli
```

JSX Compiler

This tool demonstrates how JSX syntax is desugared into native JavaScript.

Live JSX Editor

```
var CommentsList = React.createClass({
  render: function() {
    return (
      <ul>
        <li>ReactJS</li>
        <li>JSX</li>
        <li>
          <input type="text" />
          <button>Add</button>
        </li>
      </ul>
    );
  }
});
```

```
var CommentsList = React.createClass({displayName: "CommentsList",
  render: function() {
    return (
      React.createElement("ul", null,
        React.createElement("li", null, "ReactJS"),
        React.createElement("li", null, "JSX"),
        React.createElement("li", null,
          React.createElement("input", {type: "text"}),
          React.createElement("button", null, "Add")
        )
      )
    );
  }
});
```

☐ Enable ES6 transforms (--harmony)

We can also use the node npm package that the ReactJS team built to transform your JSX files. First, you need to install the `react-tools` NPM package with:

```
npm install react-tools -g
```

This will install `react-tools` globally. All you need now is to run the following command from your project folder:

```
jsx --watch src/ build/
```

This command transforms every script in the `src` folder and puts it in the `build` folder. The `watch` parameter makes this tool run the same command every time a file changes in the `src` folder. This is a very useful tool because you're using node to bundle your frontend code.

If you're familiar with task runner tools such as Grunt or Gulp, they also have JSX transformer packages that can be installed with `npm` as well. In this case, they provide more options that can fit better in our deployment/building process, mainly if you already use one of them. It's not the purpose of this book to dive into Grunt or Gulp. In order to configure and install them, you can follow their guidelines in the following links: Details of these are covered in *Chapter 9*, *Preparing Your Code for Deployment*.

- Grunt – `https://www.gruntjs.com`
- Gulp – `https://www.gulpjs.com`

Both sites have a `/plugins` page where you can search for available plugins. The following are the links of these download tools:

- Grunt React task — `https://www.npmjs.com/package/grunt-react`
- Gulp React task — `https://www.npmjs.com/package/gulp-react/`

They work much the same as do the React tools. We are going to use the `transformer` script file that is placed in `head` the element of our HTML page for the next examples, as this is easier to do. In *Chapter 9*, *Preparing Your Code for Deployment*, we are going to use `webpack` and `gulp` as the `npm` packages to transform our JSX code and prepare it for deployment.

The ReactJS anatomy

Before going any further into JSX, we need to understand some basic rules to build ReactJS components. First, we're going to detail the basic methods that you've already used to create and render components. Then, we'll move to some rules to create them, and finally, we'll talk about children components.

Creating a component

In order to create a component, we need to use the React.createClass function. ReactJS components are basically classes. This method returns a ReactJS component definition that has a method named render, which is mandatory to implement. There are many other methods to configure your component and change its behavior that we are going to cover throughout the book.

This is an example of how to use the createClass and render method:

```
var HelloMessage = React.createClass({
  render: function() {
    return (
      <h1>Have a good day!</h1>
    );
  }
});
```

 It's a good practice to name all the classes and components in PascalCase. In addition to being a common pattern in JavaScript, it also helps to distinguish them from other variables.

Rendering a component

Once you have your component definition, as seen in our last example, the HelloMessage component, we can render it with the render method of ReactJS. It requires the component definition and the target location, where the component will be rendered. Let's demonstrate this with the following:

```
React.render(<HelloMessage />, document.body);
```

In the code mentioned earlier, you could change document.body with any other element in your page. For example, you could use the document object method document.getElementById('id') to find an element by its ID or any other helper that returns a DOM element. In the specific ID of the DOM (id in this case), the React component will be rendered.

Maximum number of roots

It's not possible to return more than one element in the `render` method. Not for now, as they say in official ReactJS docs at `http://facebook.github.io/react/tips/maximum-number-of-jsx-root-nodes.html`:

```
var HelloMessage = React.createClass({
  render: function() {
    return (
      <h1>Have a good day!</h1>
      <h2>This is going to BREAK!</h2>

    );
  }
});
```

The ReactJS library will throw a strange error that doesn't address clearly that you have more than one element being rendered. Therefore, take care to not do this; otherwise, you can get stuck trying to find the problem.

When you have more than one element being represented by a ReactJS component, you must wrap them in a single parent element. The next example demonstrates this:

```
var HelloMessage = React.createClass({
  render: function() {
    return (
      <div>
        <h1>Have a good day!</h1>
        <h2>This is NOT going to BREAK!</h2>
      </div>
    );
  }
});
```

You can use whichever valid HTML element you want that supports children elements. It is also possible to render a custom ReactJS component that has children support (more about this in the next section).

This is one of the reasons to choose a good text editor and a good linter/lint package that can watch your code and warn you whenever you make a mistake.

Children components

If there is a really necessary thing when you talk about creating reusable user interfaces, it has to do with nesting components. This way you can better structure and separate concerns of your application. It's a pretty common thing to do on web world as well, as HTML has this feature built-in. As you could see in the last section and earlier examples of this book, ReactJS supports this feature as well and JSX syntax makes it very straightforward.

Let's say that you have a `Header` component and you want to place other components inside. ReactJS allows this and includes support for placing other ReactJS components:

```
var Header = React.createClass({
  render: function () {
    return (
      <nav>
        <h1>This is my awesome app</h1>
        {this.props.children}
      </nav>
    );
  }
});


var Clock = React.createClass({
  render: function () {
    return <span>{new Date().toLocaleTimeString()}</span>;
  }
});


var ComponentThatHasHeader = React.createClass({
  render: function () {
    return(
      <Header>
        <h2>This is my another component</h2>
        <Clock />
      </Header>
    );
  }
});


React.render(<ComponentThatHasHeader />, document.body);
```

You can use either built-in components, such as h2, or custom components, such as the Clock component, described here. In this example, the expression {this.props.children} will be considered as a JavaScript array. If there was a single component like the one mentioned later, it will be addressed as a JavaScript object instead of an array. This saves array allocation, but we should be careful and not try to iterate it or check for its length:

```
<Header>
    <Clock />
</Header>
```

Supported attributes

Some HTML attributes conflict with JavaScript reserved words, and as ReactJS elements are basically JavaScript objects, such attributes have a different name in ReactJS to match the DOM API specification:

- The class is className

- for is htmlFor

- Custom attributes, such as data-* and aria-*, are supported by ReactJS. There is an official list of HTML attributes supported, as follows:

```
accept acceptCharset accessKey action allowFullScreen allowTransparency
alt async autoComplete autoPlay cellPadding cellSpacing charSet checked
classID className cols colSpan content contentEditable contextMenu
controls coords crossOrigin data dateTime defer dir disabled download
draggable encType form formAction formEncType formMethod formNoValidate
formTarget frameBorder height
```

```
hidden href hrefLang htmlFor httpEquiv icon id label lang list loop
manifest marginHeight marginWidth max maxLength media mediaGroup method
min multiple muted name noValidate open pattern placeholder poster preload
radioGroup readOnly rel required role rows rowSpan sandbox scope scrolling
seamless selected shape size sizes span spellCheck src srcDoc srcSet start
step style tabIndex target title type useMap value width wmode
```

At the time of writing this book, this is available at http://facebook.github.io/react/docs/tags-and-attributes.html.

Supported elements

The official ReactJS website also provides a list of supported elements. ReactJS supports mostly all HTML elements. A comprehensive list of all the supported elements are given on their website, `https://facebook.github.io/react/docs/tags-and-attributes.html`.

HTML elements

The following are the elements that are supported. There are many more to the list as well:

a	abbr	address	area
article	aside	audio	b
base	bdi	bdo	big
blockquote	body	br	button
canvas	caption	cite	code
col	colgroup	data	datalist
dd	del	details	dfn
dialog	div	dl	dt
em	embed	footer	fieldset
figcaption	figure	form	h4
h1	h2	h3	h5
h6	head	header	hr
html	i	iframe	img
input	ins	kbd	keygen
label	legend	li	link
main	map	mark	menu
menuitem	meta	meter	nav
noscript	object	ol	optgroup
option	output	p	param
picture	pre	progress	q
rp	rt	ruby	s
samp	script	section	select
small	source	span	strong
style	sub	summary	sup
table	tbody	td	textarea
tfoot	thead	time	tr
track	u	ul	video
wbr			

SVG elements

The following are some of the supported SVG elements:

```
circle defs ellipse g line linearGradient mask path pattern polygon
polyline radialGradient rect stop svg text tspan
```

Learning JSX and Gotchas

Now it's time to master JSX and learn some Gotchas. You're going to learn some basic concepts to build ReactJS UI components using JSX. It includes practices when writing expressions, conditions, and creating lists of components. It will also walk you through how JSX differs from HTML (because it's not HTML) in some aspects.

Expressions

Consider the following code:

```
var Clock = React.createClass({
  render: function () {
    var today = new Date();
    return <h1>The time is { today.toLocaleTimeString() }</h1>;
  }
});

React.render(<Clock />, document.body);
```

JSX understands the curly braces {} whenever you want to put JavaScript code within your presentation code.

In the next example, let's improve our Clock component by supporting greetings depending on what the time is.

In the highlighted code mentioned later, if the current hour is lesser than 4, it should return day, and if the hour is greater than 4 but less than 18, it should return night:

```
var GreetingsClock = React.createClass({
  render: function () {
    var today = new Date();
    return <h1>Hey! Have a good { today.getHours() > 4 && today.
getHours() < 18 ? 'day' : 'night' }!</h1>;
  }
});

React.render(<GreetingsClock />, document.body);
```

As you can see, it's possible to make a ternary within the curly braces. You can place any valid JavaScript code within them. It's more common to create a variable and address it to the result of this expression before rendering your component. This makes your code cleaner and more readable.

In the next example, we will demonstrate how to render a component based on a condition. There are two components, one for login and the other for the user details. It depends on the fact that if the user is logged in, the user details component will be shown; otherwise, the login one will be rendered. The code to detect whether the user is logged in or not will be skipped, as this is just to demonstrate how to put rendering logic inside ReactJS components using JSX syntax:

```
var loginPane;
if (IsUserLoggedIn) {
  loginPane = <UserDetails />
} else {
  loginPane = <LoginButton />
}

React.render(loginPane, document.getElementById('login-div'));
```

You can put this code inside a component that contains all other components as children, as demonstrated in the next example:

```
var App = React.createClass({
  render: function () {
    var loginPane;
    if (isUserLoggedIn) {
      loginPane = <UserDetails />
    } else {
      loginPane = <LoginButton />
    }

    return (
      <nav>
        <Home />
        {loginPane}
      </nav>
    )
  }
});

React.render(<App />, document.body);
```

Properties/attributes

Properties allow you to customize your components, and JSX supports them in a very similar way to HTML elements. You can pass properties to ReactJS elements and get them before rendering the component. This is a very key fundamental of ReactJS, and you're going to learn how to work with them using JSX. In the next chapter, we'll dive into how properties work and discuss good practices on how to use them.

Consider the following example:

```
var HelloMessage = React.createClass({
  render: function() {
    return (
        <h1>Have a good day {this.props.name}</h1>
    );
  }
});
```

In order to render this component, you have to pass properties to it, just like we do in HTML elements:

```
React.render(<HelloMessage name="reader" />, document.body);
```

You can also use expressions inside properties:

```
React.render(<HelloMessage name={1 + 1} />, document.body);
```

If we don't set the properties (name) required by a component, in our last example, it will be rendered as an empty string. Thus, if there are expressions trying to access that property, then it will throw an error.

Transferring properties

Passing properties throughout your component hierarchy is a very common thing to do in ReactJS. You can think of properties as a way of making your component dynamic, and because you are splitting your components into smaller ones, you need an efficient way to pass incoming configuration and data to them.

Consider the following nested components:

```
var UserInfo = React.createClass({
  render: function () {
    return (
      <section id="user-section">
        <h2>{this.props.firstName} {this.props.lastName}</h2>
        <h3>{this.props.cityName} / {this.props.stateName}</h3>
      </section>
```

```
            );
         }
      });

      var App = React.createClass({
        render: function () {
          return (
            <div>
              <h1>My Awesome app!</h1>
              <UserInfo firstName={this.props.firstName}
                        lastName={this.props.lastName}
                        cityName={this.props.cityName}
                        stateName={this.props.stateName} />
            </div>
          );
        }
      });

      React.render(<App firstName="Learning"
                        lastName="ReactJS"
                        cityName="Florianopolis"
                        stateName="Santa Catarina" />, document.body);
```

As we can see, it's possible to pass properties to child components. If you have lots of properties to pass on, it becomes a tedious task to do and your code will get very messy.

Fortunately, you can transfer them in a fancy way that JSX provides us. All you're going to do is to change your App component, so it can pass all its properties on that were received by the React.render function. This is done using the spread operator {...this.props} notation that JSX understands. The following is an example explaining this:

```
      var App = React.createClass({
        render: function () {
          return (
            <div>
              <h1>My Awesome app!</h1>
              <UserInfo {...this.props} />
            </div>
          );
        }
      });
```

Much clearer! However, there is still a problem with that solution. It can override properties on your subcomponents. Let's take another example, imagine you have a property named `name`, and you want to pass it along. Some elements, basically HTML input elements, have this attribute to define their names inside forms. If you change it, it can result in unexpected consequences. Another example is the input checkbox or radio. Both have an attribute named `checked`, which defines whether the control will be visually checked. If you pass on a property named `checked`, it'd definitely result in a bad behavior. In order to avoid this, it's possible to skip some properties using the same notation. You just need to specify them as:

```
var App = React.createClass({
  render: function () {
    var {name} = this.props;

    return (
      <div>
        <h1>My Awesome app! {name}</h1>

      </div>
    );
  }
});
```

Everything that comes before the three dots, . . ., will be considered as separated variables, and the one that comes after the three dots, . . ., will be addressed to an array with all the remaining properties. This is an experimental ES6 (ECMA Script) syntax, and there are some ways you can transform that code into plain JavaScript. Details of ES6 are covered later in *Chapter 5, Component Lifecycle and Newer ECMA Script in React*.

By looking through `https://www.npmjs.com/package/react-tools`, you can find the details of the different options you can pass with the JSX Transformer.

`--harmony`: turns on JS transformations such as ES6 classes and so on.

Thus, the ES6 syntax will be transformed into ES5-compatible syntaxes.

The first way is to put an extra argument named `harmony` on your HTML `script` element so that the transformer will know that it's going to need to understand the new version of ECMAScript in order to transform. This is how your script tag should look like:

```
<script type="text/jsx;harmony=true"
src="properties.js"></script>
```

ES6 (also known as Harmony) is a version (actual is ES5) of ECMAScript that is a standardized scripting language. The most known implementation of this standard is the JavaScript language, but there are many others.

You can also use the `react-tools` node package. This exposes a command named `jsx` that can transform your files offline. In order to use it, you're going to need to run this command from any console tool within your application's folder:

```
jsx -x jsx --harmony . .
```

The `-x` option allows you to specify the syntax to search for. In our examples, we are creating the `.jsx` files, but you could also do that with the `.js` files that have the JSX code inside. The `--harmony` option is the same from the last example. It tells the transformer to understand ES6/ES7 features of the JavaScript language.

You can find out how to install `react-tools` in the earlier section *Tools for transforming JSX*, as discussed earlier in this chapter.

The reason to use the `.jsx` files is it facilitates text editors to match an installed syntax highlight without the need for configuring it.

Mutating properties

Once your React component is rendered, it's not recommended to mutate its properties. This is considered an antipattern. Properties are immutable, and they roughly represent your presentation once it's rendered. Consider the following code:

```
var HelloMessage = React.createClass({
  render: function () {
    return <h1>Hello {this.props.name}</h1>;
  }
});

var component = <HelloMessage />;
component.props.name = 'Testing';

React.render(component, document.body);
```

Although this work has a great chance to end up in unexpected results. The component's state is the only way to mutate data in a ReactJS component. The next two chapters cover details of props and states and when and where they should be used. States and properties are both keys in how ReactJS core works.

Comments

JSX allows you to place comments in your code; they differ in syntax depending on whether you're placing them in a nested component or outside of it. Follow the next example:

```
var Header = React.createClass({
  render: function () {
    return (
      //this is the nav
      <nav>
        {/* this is the nav */}
        <h1>This is my awesome app</h1>
        {this.props.children}
      </nav>
    );
  }
});
```

When within a nested component, you just need to wrap your comment with curly braces (like expressions).

Component style

You can either style your component with the `className` or `style` properties. The `className` property works in the same way HTML class does and the `style` property applies inline style to your component, also similar to HTML. It's up to you to choose one that you prefer; both of them have an easy way to be handled in ReactJS, mainly when you need it to be dynamic.

Style

Whenever you want to apply style to your component, you can use a JavaScript object to do so. This object's properties must match the DOM style specification, such as `height`, `width`, and so on. See the example here:

```
var StyledComponent = React.createClass({
  render: function () {
    return (
      <div style={{height: 50, width: 50, backgroundColor:
      'red'}}>
        I have style!
      </div>
```

```
      );
    }
});
```

```
React.render(<StyledComponent />, document.body);
```

This is going to render a red small square `div` with text inside. You can move this style object to a variable and dynamically set that depending on your component properties or state. Properties and state will be discussed later in *Chapter 3, Breaking Your UI into Components* and *Chapter 4, Stateful Components and Events*, respectively. For demonstration purposes, this is how you move this style object out of the component markup:

```
render: function () {
  var style = { height: 50, width: 50, backgroundColor: 'red' };

  return (
    <div style={style}>
      I have style!
    </div>
  );
}
```

When you have styles where names are separated by dashes -, you need to write them in CamelCase, as you can see in our example for the `backgroundColor` style property earlier. Vendor prefixes other than `ms` should begin with a capital letter; for example, `WebkitTransition` will be transformed to `webkit-transition` and `msTransition` will be transformed to `ms-transition`. All other vendor names must begin with a capital letter.

CSS classes

In order to add CSS classes to your component, you need to specify the `className` property for them: `<component className="class1 class2" />`. Unfortunately, `className` doesn't support an object literal like style does. If we want to change them dynamically, you need to concatenate strings or use classnames from `https://github.com/JedWatson/classnames`. Consider the following example:

```
var ClassedComponent = React.createClass({
  render: function ()   {
    var className = 'initial-class';
    if (this.props.isUrgent) {
```

```
        className += ' urgent';
    }

    return (
      <div className={className}>
        I have class!
      </div>
    );
  }
});
```

```
React.render(<ClassedComponent isUrgent={true} />, document.body);
```

In this example, we are concatenating strings, but this is a very tedious task to do, and it might lead to mistakes and errors. There is a class manipulation utility provided by ReactJS add-ons. If we are using ReactJS library script file, you should get the one that comes with add-ons embedded, as mentioned in downloading the ReactJS section on *Chapter 1, Getting Started with ReactJS*:

```
<script src="http://fb.me/react-with-addons-0.12.2.js"></script>
```

If you are using node or other CommonJS/AMD package to require ReactJS dependency, you can reference add-ons through requiring `require('react/addons')` instead of just requiring React.

Now, let's check how our code functions using this utility code:

```
var Button = React.createClass({
  // ...
  render () {
    var btnClass = 'btn';
    if (this.state.isPressed) btnClass += ' btn-pressed';
    else if (this.state.isHovered) btnClass += ' btn-over';
    return <button className={btnClass}>{this.props.label}</button>;
  }
});
```

Try changing the `isUrgent` property and see that the class property changes when you reload the page.

Summary

In this chapter, you learned what JSX is, its syntax, and why it is necessary. We looked into some examples and how to build them using JSX. We covered very basic principles of ReactJS and how JSX helps you build components faster, easy to read, and reasonable.

In the next chapter, we are going to dive into ReactJS properties and how to break the UI into smaller components. You are going to learn it by creating a small application that will consume the Facebook Open Graph API and list your liked pages.

3
Working with Properties

In this chapter, we will be exploring how to work with ReactJS properties. We're also going to learn how to integrate ReactJS with an external API (Facebook Open-Graph API) and render incoming data in a set of components. This chapter will cover the following items:

- Component properties
- Component's data flow
- Configuring and consuming Facebook Open-Graph API
- Creating a ReactJS component and list data from API

Component properties

In the *Chapter 2, Exploring JSX and ReactJS Anatomy*, we talked a lot about ReactJS properties and used them throughout our examples, but so far, we've just used them like HTML properties. They play a role that is far beyond that. It's common to use them to pass data through your components tree that defines your view; to pass configuration properties that come from parent components; to pass callbacks for user input, UI/custom events that need to be triggered outside, and so on.

Properties of a ReactJS component can't be changed once the component is rendered in the DOM.

Properties define the declarative interface of the component. In a `h1` element that renders a name property, for example, you can't change this name once it's rendered, unless you create another instance of the component and render it in the same place in the DOM, replacing the old rendered component.

```
var GreetingsComponent = React.createClass({
  render: function() {
    return (
      <h1>Hello {this.props.name}!</h1>
    );
  }
});
```

```
React.render(<GreetingsComponent name="Readers" />,
document.body);
// instead of rendering on the body rendering in a specific id
('app)
React.render(<GreetingsComponent name="Folks" />,
document.getElemenById('app'));
```

This happens because ReactJS represents the state of your component at any point in time and not only at initialization. Consider the following example:

```
var CustomInput = React.createClass({
  render: function() {
    return (
      <input type="text" value={this.props.text} />
    );
  }
});
```

```
React.render(<CustomInput text="Learning ReactJS" />,
document.body);
```

The input text being rendered is considered to be a controlled component because it won't change the value even if you try typing on it. If we don't specify the `value` property of the input then it is considered to be an uncontrolled component. Controlled components have their data updated via the ReactJS data flow and component cycle. However, if you did not specify the value property, the value property would not be controlled by ReactJS and would exist externally to the ReactJS data flow. The correct way to change the value from forms inputs or other components is to set up `state` for them, which will be described in more detail in the next chapter.

Data flow with properties

One of the ReactJS fundamentals and best practices is to pass data to nested components through properties. In that way, the children components can have the single responsibility of rendering only what they have to render and pass the job to further components, thus ensuring the separation of concerns. It's also used for configuring nested components so that the ones at the top of the hierarchy can say what particular aspects the children components should have, just by passing properties. It's also common to define functions on parent nodes and pass them to children as a callback to be triggered whenever the child component wants, improving the component reusability and testability.

Let's demonstrate a small example simulating a static to-do list. The list is split into small components that render only the necessary and pass properties down to children components, defining the whole functionality of the view. This is what it is going to render at the end:

- Write this book with love <3   Remove
- Learn how to create isomorphic web apps   Remove
- Study FLUX architecture   ✓ Remove

We're going to break our view into smaller components and will start doing it from the innermost one to the topmost one. Before we start, let's discuss a little more about each component and its role in view:

- TaskList – This component represents a list (the ul element) that accepts an array of tasks to be rendered. It iterates through the tasks array creating a TaskItem component. Along with passing the task details through a property, to be rendered in the TaskItem component, it also passes some function callbacks that, for now, will just fake some operations to simplify the demonstration.

- TaskItem – This component represent a single task (the li element) that renders the task name, an input checkbox representing whether the task is completed, and a button to remove the task. Again, the input and the button will just log some text to simplify the demonstration.

The TaskItem component should look like this:

```
var TaskItem = React.createClass({
  render: function() {
```

```
        var task = this.props.task;

        return (
          <li>
            <span>{task.name}</span>
            <div>
              <input type="checkbox"

                  if (task.completed) {
                  checked = "checked";
            } else {
                  checked =   "";
            }

                onChange={this.props.markTaskComplete

              <button
              onClick={this.props.removeTask}>Remove</button>
            </div>
          </li>
        );
      }
    });
```

The `TaskList` component should be as follows:

```
var TaskList = React.createClass({
  markTaskCompleted: function (task) {
    console.log('task ' + task.name + ' has been
    completed!');
  },

  removeTask: function (task) {
    console.log('task ' + task.name + ' has been
    removed!');
  },

  render: function() {
/*The map() method creates a new array with the results of
calling a provided    function on every element in this
array. Here this.props.tasks will create a new array, with
the callback as task. (source  HYPERLINK
"https://developer.mozilla.org/en-
US/docs/Web/JavaScript/Reference/Global_Objects/Array/map"h
ttps://developer.mozilla.org/en-
US/docs/Web/JavaScript/Reference/Global_Objects/Array/map
HYPERLINK "").  */
```

```
        var taskItems = this.props.tasks.map(function (task) {
          return <TaskItem task={task}
                           markTaskCompleted={this.markTaskCompleted}
                           removeTask={this.removeTask} />;
        }.bind(this));
    /*The bind() method creates a new function that, when
    called, has its this keyword set to the provided value, with
    a given sequence of arguments (if any) this (source  HYPERLINK
    "https://developer.mozilla.org/en-
    US/docs/Web/JavaScript/Reference/Global_Objects/Function/bi
    nd"https://developer.mozilla.org/en-
    US/docs/Web/JavaScript/Reference/Global_Objects/Function/bi
    nd). .bind is used in this case to simply more arguments
    and esnsure a parent chind relationship, which is not new
    to ReactJS but a concenpt of core Javascript. */
        return (
          <ul>
            {taskItems}
          </ul>
        );
      }
    });
```

The task list has a bit more functionality and code. It takes care of rendering the list of tasks and handles operations on it. This is a very common pattern in ReactJS, to maintain the control of your model objects in a single place that is, of course, if it's responsibility for doing so. In a more complicated scenario, you would have some "controllers" or "containers" (as they like to call them in the ReactJS community), each one having its own task and encapsulating what they are responsible for. Thus, all of the containers are having their own responsibility and not interfering with each other.

There is just one missing part in our static task list example, which is to render the component in an HTML element:

```
var tasks = [
  { name: 'Write this book with love <3', completed: false },
  { name: 'Learn isomorphic web apps', completed: false },
  { name: 'Study FLUX architecture', completed: true },
];

React.render(<TaskList tasks={tasks} />, document.body);
```

We're passing some static tasks to the list to explain how properties work and some practices on how to use them. We think that small examples as to-do/tasks/hello-worlds don't represent the real-world problems that we face day by day; although they are great for starting to learn a tool functionality, they fail when you try to make more reasonable examples that have asynchronous operations, deal with outside APIs, authentication, and so on. For that reason, the following topics will cover how to set up our real scenario applications using Facebook API (also known as Open-Graph API), logins into Facebook, and lists that a logged-in user likes.

Configuring Facebook Open-Graph API

In the following sections, we're going to learn more about Facebook Open-Graph API and configure it so we can start crafting some code to build our awesome application.

What it is and how to configure it

Facebook Open-Graph API is a service for getting, editing, and adding common Facebook resources. Some of its functionalities that you can use in your own application are: login; request user-specific resource permissions such as manage events, post to friends walls, and the list goes on. It has a bunch of functionalities that you can use and integrate your app with. One of the main functionalities used by third-party applications is, of course, the login integration. You can use it just as a login platform, for instance, if you don't want or don't have time to build one.

 The API documentation is provided at `https://developers.facebook.com/` and it's recommended that you check this out.

If you want to test some requests to their API, without having to start developing an application from scratch, you can use a very useful tool called *Graph API Explorer*. It's commonly used for testing out an endpoint before developing it or just checking how the response JSON result is returned. Graph API Explorer can be found at the **Tools & Support** menu item at the top header. This is what the tool looks like:

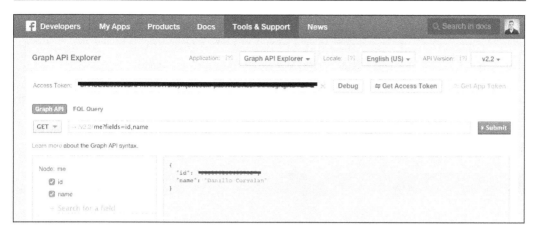

Most of the resources available on Facebook Open-Graph API require authorization. Just a few are available without having to provide an **access token**. An access token is a kind of ticket used by your application to act on the user's behalf, so you can get or submit data. Basically, you ask Facebook for some user's permissions; Facebook opens a popup asking the user to log in and shows the permissions your app is requesting; once the user allows them, Facebook will send back the user information/object to your page with the generated access token. From that time on, you have access to other Open-Graph API resources that your app needs. You just have to provide this token to every subsequent request you make. This is how *OAuth* authorization standards work but this book will not cover OAuth in detail, as it is not the purpose of this book.

 You can find more details about *OAuth* at `http://oauth.net/2/`.

In Graph API Explorer, you can get an access token by clicking on the button **Get Access Token**. This will open a popup with a bunch of permissions that your operation can use. Once you have selected the permissions you want, Graph API Explorer will show a popup requesting you to confirm the permissions requested. This process generates a new access token that allows you to make request actions to those restricted resources. Try checking out the `user_likes` permission and requesting your user's list of likes through the endpoint `/me/likes`:

You will probably see a JSON result in the box below the **Submit** button.

This works very well when in Graph API Explorer but this is used just for testing purposes. In order to make that work, we have to create an application (APP-ID) at the Facebook developers site. This follows the OAuth standards specification and allows the user, who is logging in to your app, to know more about your application before granting access. In order to create an application in Facebook and obtain this APP-ID, go to the **My Apps** menu at the header of the page; there will be an option for creating a new app.

At the time of writing this book, the Facebook Open-Graph API recommended version was v.2.2.

Creating an app-id on the Facebook developers site

When you click the **Add a New App** button shown in the preceding image, Facebook will ask you which type of application you need.

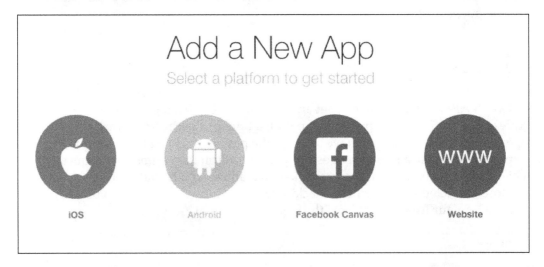

Choose the **Website** option, which indicates our app is going to run in a separate web page with no Facebook content around. After that, give it a fancy, original, and unpredictable name as I did: `learning-reactjs`. Once it's done, you will be redirected to the app details and configuration page that looks something like this:

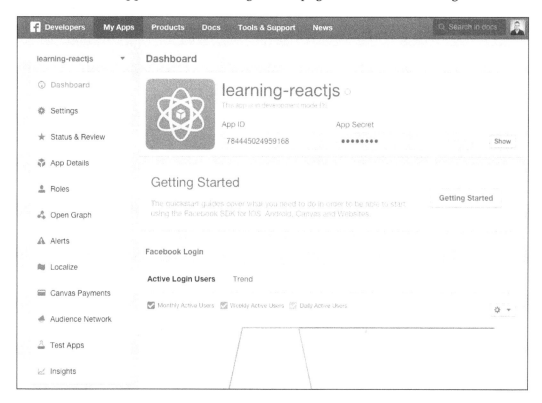

Yay! We have our app-id ready; now we can use it to make request calls to Facebook Open-Graph API.

One important thing to note is that some permissions require further analysis from Facebook before going into production. As we are going to use this just for getting the data of our own user, it's OK. If you try to log in with a different user, it won't be possible as the `user_likes` permission requires your application to be submitted to analysis and doing that takes lots of time and should be done just in case you want to put your application into production.

Open-Graph JavaScript SDK

Facebook Open-Graph API provides SDKs for common programming languages to ease the pain of consuming their resources. The JavaScript SDK can be found at `https://developers.facebook.com/docs/javascript`. Their documentation (`https://developers.facebook.com/docs/javascript/quickstart/v2.5`) is comprehensive and they have tutorials such as logging in, working with multiple requests, and so on. If you're considering taking an advanced course in learning Open-Graph API using JavaScript SDK, it is worth taking a look afterward.

Just to recap what we're about to do: we're going to create a simple HTML page that will load the Facebook JavaScript SDK. After that, we're going to log in to Facebook and request our logged-in user list of likes and pass it to a ReactJS component, which we will also create, through properties.

The Facebook JavaScript SDK needs to be loaded in the background, without the waiting time (asynchronously) after the page finishes loading. In order to do that, we need to create a `script` HTML element, put its `src` (source) attribute to point to the SDK script, and, finally, insert that into the DOM. Fortunately, the SDK page has an example ready to use and you just need to replace the `APP-ID` property within it. We are going to use their example. This is what the script looks like:

```
<script>
  window.fbAsyncInit = function() {
    FB.init({
      appId       : '784445024959168',
      xfbml       : true,
      version     : 'v2.2'
    });
  };

  (function(d, s, id){
     var js, fjs = d.getElementsByTagName(s)[0];
     if (d.getElementById(id)) {return;}
     js = d.createElement(s); js.id = id;

     js.src = "//connect.facebook.net/en_US/sdk/debug.js";
     fjs.parentNode.insertBefore(js, fjs);
   }(document, 'script', 'facebook-jssdk'));
</script>
```

 `window.fbAsyncInit` is an initialization function with your Facebook `appId` and other details.

Once the asynchronous initialization is done, if the concerned element is found, then JavaScript(js) connects with `//connect.facebook.net/en_US/sdk/debug.js`.

We need to change the `appId` parameter to t Facebook-app-id.

So, let's get started by creating an `index.html` file inside a separate folder to organize things. The page will be like this:

```html
<html>
  <head>
    <title>Rahh</title>
    <script src="http://fb.me/react-0.12.2.js"></script>
    <script src="http://fb.me/JSXTransformer-0.12.2.js"></script>
  </head>
  <body>

    <h1>Facebook User's list of likes</h1>
    <a onClick='logout()' href='#'>Logout</a>
    <div id="main"></div>

    <script>
      window.fbAsyncInit = function() {
        FB.init({
          appId      : '784445024959168',
          xfbml      : true,
          version    : 'v2.2'
        });

        checkLoginStatusAndLoadUserLikes();
      };

      (function(d, s, id){
         var js, fjs = d.getElementsByTagName(s)[0];
         if (d.getElementById(id)) {return;}
         js = d.createElement(s); js.id = id;
         //js.src = "//connect.facebook.net/en_US/sdk.js";
         js.src = "//connect.facebook.net/en_US/sdk/debug.js";
         fjs.parentNode.insertBefore(js, fjs);
       }(document, 'script', 'facebook-jssdk'));
    </script>

    <script type="text/jsx" src="index.jsx"></script>
  </body>
</html>
```

We are commenting the `js.src` line and duplicating it with a debug JavaScript file. This helps with finding errors and debugging your script.

A **Content Delivery Network** or **Content Distribution Network** (**CDN**) is a globally distributed network of proxies. Source: https://en.wikipedia.org/wiki/Server_(computing)

Servers are deployed in multiple data centers. Source: https://en.wikipedia.org/wiki/Data_center

The goal of a CDN is to serve content to end users with high availability and high performance. Source https://en.wikipedia.org/wiki/Content_delivery_network

First, we need to reference ReactJS dependencies and we are referencing the CDN version ones to make it easier to demonstrate and for learning purposes. After referencing the dependencies, we create some HTML elements, a title, a logout anchor to log out from Facebook, and a `div` that will be the host for the ReactJS component to be rendered. Later, we configure the Facebook Open-Graph JavaScript SDK as explained before, but with one extra command, `checkLoginStatusAndLoadUserLikes();`, that will be explained soon. Lastly, we reference our `index.jsx` file that will contain the magic to make it all happen.

We put the `checkLoginStatusAndLoadUserLikes` call within the `fbAsyncInit` function because the Open-Graph SDK JavaScript triggers that function once it is loaded, so this is the right place to call Open-Graph API calls. Continuing with our development, inside our `index.jsx` file, let's implement the `logout` and `checkLoginStatusAndLoadUserLikes` functions and test it out in order to see the Facebook integration working.

The `logout` function should be as simple as this:

```
function logout() {
   FB.logout();
}
```

This will just log the user out of Facebook, requiring him to log in again. As we'll keep it simple, for learning purposes, we're not going to handle the scenario where the user logs in and out to manage the list of likes when these events happen in sequence. So, let's implement our `checkLoginStatusAndLoadUserLikes` function:

```
function checkLoginStatusAndLoadUserLikes() {
   FB.login(function(response) {
      console.log('We are live!!');
   });
}
```

This is a very straightforward code as well. Every call made by the Open-Graph JavaScript SDK will be done asynchronously, so we have to provide a functions callback that will be triggered once the request made to Facebook API returns with the response. In this code, we're going to log in to the console once we've logged in to the app. This process will call a Facebook login popup:

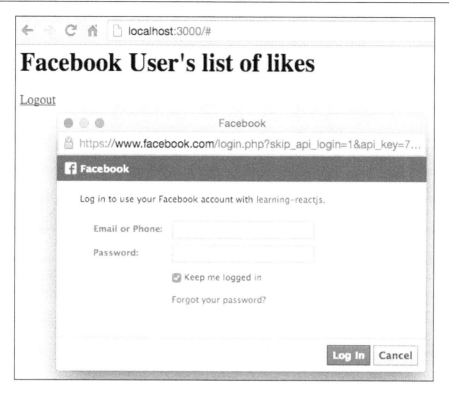

Try it out! Load the screen and once logged in, click the logout anchor and reload the page again, check out the console from your browser, and see the log we've printed. The following image shows the login popup.

In order to make it work in localhost:3000, it's necessary that you run the Python SimpleHTTPServer command from inside the code folder, python -m SimpleHTTPServer. For more details about this command and other ways of running your app, check *Chapter 1, Getting Started with ReactJS*.

You can also make it work by using the following command:

npm -g install httpster

httpster: Is a simple http server to run the static content. In chrome browser the index.html file sometime's doesn't render due to X-origin error. Hence running this webserver from your application directory, will be easier to test your application in Chrome. Just run the command httpster from your application's root directory.

By Default the server runs in port 3333, thus localhost:3333 in the browsers should render the index.html page of your application.

Now that we have our integration working, let's get this list of likes for the logged-in user. Change your `checkLoginStatusAndLoadUserLikes` function to be like so:

```
function checkLoginStatusAndLoadUserLikes() {
  FB.getLoginStatus(function(response) {
    if (response.status === 'connected') {
      loadUserAndLikes();
    } else {
      loginAndLoadUserLikes();
    }
  });
}
```

The first step is to check out where the user is already logged in. Calling the `FB.getLoginStatus` function can do this. Inside the callback function, the parameter passed represents the response from the API. This response contains information about the login status for the user. This will be a very common parameter as other API calls also return a response object back to your callback function. The status that represents that the user has authorized the app and has successfully logged in is the `connected` one. If the user is already logged in, we just call the `loadUserAndLikes` function, but if it's not connected then it calls another function that will log in and then call the API to load the user's list of likes.

The function `loginAndLoadUserLikes` should be as follows:

```
function loginAndLoadUserLikes() {
  FB.login(function(response) {
    loadUserAndLikes();
  }, {scope: 'user_likes'});
}
```

The login functionality has been moved to this method. Once the login operation is complete then we call `loadUserAndLikes`. Notice that we now pass an object at the end of the login function call `{scope: 'user_likes'}`; this object represents the scope/permissions on Facebook, as required by our applicaton. In the following example, within the first function call (`loadUserAndLikes`), the `userResponse` of the logged-in user is returned. Then the API lists all the likes of that logged-in user.

The function `loadUserAndLikes` should look like this:

```
function loadUserAndLikes() {
  FB.api('/me', function(userResponse) {
    console.log(1, userResponse);
    FB.api('/me/likes', function(likesResponse) {
      console.log(2, likesResponse);
    });
  });
}
```

You can have as much JavaScript code as you want inside JSX files. It's not a specific type of file that understands only its own syntax, it just converts the places where you use JSX-specific syntax markup instead.

Notice that we are making two requests for the API: the first one will get the user details and the other will get the user's list of likes. We are logging them to the console in order to test first before we implement our ReactJS component to render it. This is what it logs out for my user:

Until now, we have explored Facebook Open-Graph API and ways to configure it. You might be wondering what it has to do with learning ReactJS? All I can say is that, in my experience, all the examples that most people try to provide when teaching a new library or framework, rely on **To-Do** apps, synchronous operations and, when they use an external. It doesn't make common integration tasks such as login. Such integration gives a better idea of how the thing being taught works when we put more realistic scenarios into place and try to make them as straightforward as possible. After finishing this example, we will have an idea about how to integrate ReactJS with your own private API, for instance.

Rendering data in a ReactJS component

We now have our data to pass to the ReactJS component we're going to create. First, let's start with the UserDetails component. This is going to show a link with the logged-in username and the source to this user Facebook page. First, remove our old logout anchor from the index.html file as this is not going to be necessary anymore. Our logout functionality will be moved to our ReactJS component instead. We'll also create another div, named user, above the main div; this new element will hold the UserDetails component. The changes in index.html should look like this:

```
<h1>Facebook User's list of likes</h1>
<div id="user"></div>
<div id="main"></div>
```

You can create the UserDetails ReactJS component at the bottom of the index.jsx file:

```
var UserDetails = React.createClass({
    handleLogout: function () {
    FB.logout(function () {
      alert("You're logged out, refresh the page in order to
      login again.");
    });
    }
  render: function () {
    return (
      <section id="user-details">
        <a href={this.props.userDetails.link} target="__blank">
          {this.props.userDetails.name}
        </a>
        {' | '}
        <a href="#" onClick={this.handleLogout}>Logout</a>
      </section>
    )
  },
});
```

Now, we need to change the loadUserAndLikes function to call the React.render method, pointing it to the user HTML div element:

```
function loadUserAndLikes () {
  FB.api('/me', function (userResponse) {
    React.render(<UserDetails userDetails={userResponse} />,
    document.getElementById('user'));
```

```
    FB.api('/me/likes', function (likesResponse) {
      console.log(2, likesResponse);
    });
  });
}
```

As you can see, the `UserDetails` ReactJS component is very straightforward and basic; it works like a template and just renders data that is passed to it. Don't be disappointed with this because we're going to give this more functionality in coming chapters, such as rendering a login button when logged out, instead of asking to refresh the page, hiding the list, and showing a loading `gif` image when waiting for the SDK response. All of those features require that we deal with a state and this is going to be covered in the next chapter.

You can test it by refreshing the page, clicking the logout button, and refreshing the page again. Once you log in on Facebook, the user details should be displayed in the browser, below the title of our page.

We now need to render the user's list of likes and substitute the ugly `console.log(2, likesResponse);` command to a ReactJS render function. First, let's create our `UserLikesList` component at the bottom of the `index.jsx` file:

```
var UserLikesList = React.createClass({
  render: function() {
    var items = this.props.list.map(function (likeObject) {
      return <UserLikeItem data={likeObject} />;
    });

    return (
      <ul id="user-likes-list">
        {items}
      </ul>
    );
  }
});
```

We create an array of `UserLikeItem` components called `items` and we're rendering them inside the list `<ul>` element. The `UserLikeItem` component should look like this:

```
var UserLikeItem = React.createClass({
  render: function() {
    var data = this.props.data;

    return (
      <li>
```

```
            <img src={data.picture.data.url} title={data.name} />

            <h1>{data.name} <small>{data.category}</small></h1>
        </li>
    );
    }
});
```

We put our property data in a separate variable to avoid long names inside the component markup. Note that we are also displaying an image from the liked Facebook resource; because of that, we also need to ask that in our API call and render our component passing this list of likes:

```
function loadUserAndLikes () {
  FB.api('/me', function (userResponse) {
    React.render(<UserDetails userDetails={userResponse} />,
    document.getElementById('user'));

    var fields = { fields: 'category,name,picture.type(normal)'
    };
    FB.api('/me/likes', fields, function (likesResponse) {
      React.render(<UserLikesList list={likesResponse.data} />,
      document.getElementById('main'));
    });
  });
}
```

We've changed the loadUserAndLikes function to ask the API to also bring a picture of the liked Facebook resource. By default, it's omitted from the response.

Try it out and see if you get a list of your likes displayed in the page. It might be looking very odd because we haven't created any style. Create a style element in the index.html page for styling our list: a very basic one but just for making our example more pleasing to look at:

```
<style>
  #user-likes-list {
    list-style: none;
    padding: 5px;
    margin: 0;
  }
  #user-likes-list li {
    display: inline-block;
    width: 270px;
    margin: 5px;
    background-color: rgb(122, 174, 233);
```

```
    height: 100px;
    overflow: hidden;
  }
#user-likes-list img {
    display: inline-block;
    vertical-align: top;
    width: 100px;
  }
#user-likes-list h1 {
    font-size: 1.4em;
    display: inline-block;
    width: 160px;
    vertical-align: top;
    margin-left: 5px;
    color: rgb(20, 90, 169);
    margin: 5px 0 0 5px;
  }
#user-likes-list small {
    font-size: 0.7em;
    display: block;
    color: rgb(145, 50, 0);
    margin-top: 5px;
  }
</style>
```

Facebook User's list of likes

Danillo Corvalan | Logout

 Astronomy
Field of study

 Richard Dawkins
Author

 Neil deGrasse Tyson
Public figure

 Carl Sagan
Public figure

OK, maybe it's bad without styling. Anyway, you can always ask a designer for help!

ReactJS properties make your components configurable and changeable. As you can see, it's very straightforward to create ReactJS components and render them in your page, even in an existing one. You don't need to make the whole app support the framework or start one from scratch. You simply define what your components are, considering them as a set, avoiding big ones that are difficult to maintain, and render them somewhere in the page. Its power increases by intelligently working with stateful components, and this is our next step in learning ReactJS.

Summary

In this chapter, we've learned how to pass properties to ReactJS components and render the UI based on those components. We have also learned how to make a parent component to communicate with its children. We have seen how to configure Facebook Open-Graph API, how to integrate that with ReactJS using login functionality, and how to render the response of an API request call into a set of smaller ReactJS components.

In the next chapter, we are going to dive into stateful components and explore how to make mutable ReactJS components based on a user's input or for any other reason that requires the state to change and your UI to represent that automatically.

4
Stateful Components and Events

In this chapter, we will exploit the React states and events in detail. This chapter will cover the components that have a state, the practices to communicate between them, and how to respond to users input/events in order to have the UI reflect this state. We will develop a web page where we can update the name of our liked pages from Facebook. This also covers how the state changes your React UI having enhanced performance using the virtual DOM.

This chapter will cover the following items:

- React states
- Event ecosystem

Properties versus states in ReactJS

Let's glance through the differences between props and states in React.

Properties are declared when React components are created, while **states** are declared within the component definitions. Thus, during the component initialization phase props are declared.

- In most of the scenarios, React components take data and pass in the form of props. In the other cases, when you are required to take user input to have a server request, states are used.

- `(this.props)` is used to access parameters passed from the parent component, while `(this.state)` is used to manage dynamic data. State should be considered private data.

Exploring the state property

In the last chapter, we explored React properties (**props**). Just as components can have properties, they can also have **states**. States are primarily set to those components where it is necessary to change, for example if the component has to be updated or replaced in future. Thus, it is not mandatory to have a state for the entire component.

Components can be both stateless and stateful:

- **Stateless components** are those where only props are present, but no state is defined. Thus, there will no change in these prop values for these components within the component life cycle. The only source of static data should be presented to the component instance via the props. Thus, props are immutable data for a React component.

- **Stateful components:** Stateless components, are meant to represent any React component declared as a function that has no state and returns the same markup given the same props. As the name implies, stateful components are those where both props and states are declared. Generally, any kind of such data-change communication is done via the state change [setState(data, callback)]. The updated state is then rendered in the UI. In case of interactive apps [form submission etc] where the data changes continuously, it's necessary to have such stateful components. Otherwise, for non-interactive apps, it's advisable to have fewer stateful components, because they increase complexity and redundancy in the app.

Initializing a state

Initialization of a component state is done by the method getInitialState(), which returns an object:

```
object getInitialState()
```

The getInitialState() method is invoked once before the component is mounted. The return value will be used as the initial value of this.state

 For all the following examples, we have the same content in the index.html file. Thus, we can use the same index.html file and only change the contents of the corresponding JavaScript file based on the topic being discussed.

We can create a React stateful component as follows:

```
var FormComponent = React.createClass({
  getInitialState:function(){
    return {
      name: 'Doel',
      id: 1
    };
    },
  render : function() {
    return <div>
      My name is {this.state.name}
      and my id is {this.state.id}.
    </div>;
  }
});
React.renderComponent(
  <FormComponent />,
  document.body
);
```

 The getInitialState() method initiates the component with the values (name: Doel, id: 1), during the first render cycle. These values are persisted until the state values are changed and can be collected by running {this.state.<VALUE>}.

Setting a state

Data change in React is commonly done by invoking the method setState(data, callback), which together with the data of this.state re-renders the component. If you provide an optional callback argument, React will call it when executing this method, although usually it's not required as React keeps the UI updated.

A state is set from inside the component.

The following code shows how the state is updated/set:

```
var InterfaceComponent = React.createClass({
  getInitialState : function() {
    return {
      name : "doel"
    };
  },
  handleClick : function() {
```

```
      this.setState({
        name : "doel sengupta"
      });
    },
    render : function() {
      return <div onClick={this.handleClick}>
        hello {this.state.name}, your name is successfully updated!
      </div>;
    }
  });
  React.renderComponent(
    <InterfaceComponent />,
    document.body
  );
```

Here is what we did:

- Changed values in states are reflected only after the component is mounted.

- Mounting of the component happens when it has been passed to React.
  render(<Component />).

- Our event handler onClick calls the handleClick() function, which is
  internally calling this.state(). So when the onClick event is initialized
  on the name doel, it will change its value from doel to doel sengupta.

In the React documentation (http://facebook.github.io/react/docs/
interactivity-and-dynamic-uis.html), Facebook recommends:

- Have many stateless components to render data and a stateful component
  as parent, which passes its states to the stateless children via props.

- Essentially, the function of the stateful component is to contain the
  interaction logic and the stateless components render the data.

- The state of a component has the data that is manipulated by the
  component's event handlers.

- You should keep minimal data in this.state and perform all the
  computations within the render method. This reduces redundancy
  or storage of computed values and ensures more reliability on React's
  computational abilities.

- React components should be built within render() based on the underlying
  props and states

- Props should be essentially used as the source of truth. Any data that can be
  changed via the user's input or otherwise, should be stored in states.

Replacing a state

It's also possible to replace values in the state by using the `replaceState()` method. Let's look at an example of this:

Here's a snippet of code from `index.html`:

```
<!DOCTYPE html>
<html>
<head>
<script src="https://cdnjs.cloudflare.com/ajax/libs/react/0.14.0-
rc1/react.min.js"></script>
<script
src="https://cdnjs.cloudflare.com/ajax/libs/react/0.13.3/JSXTransf
ormer.js"></script>
    <script src="https://cdnjs.cloudflare.com/ajax/libs/
    jquery/2.1.1/jquery.min.js"></script>
  <script
  src="https://cdnjs.cloudflare.com/ajax/libs/react/0.14.0-
  rc1/react-dom.js"></script>
  <meta charset="utf-8">
  <title>My React App</title>
</head>
<body>
  <div id="myApp"></div>
    <script type="text/jsx", src="replace_state.js"></script>
</body>
</html>
```

Here's the code for `replace_state.js`:

```
//calling replaceSet() method
var FormComponent = React.createClass({
  getInitialState : function() {
    return {
      first_name : "michael",
      last_name : "jackson"
    };
  },
  handleClick : function() {
    this.replaceState({
      last_name : "jordan"
    });
  },
  render : function() {
    return <div onClick={this.handleClick}>
```

```
            Hi {this.first_name + " " + this.state.last_name }
        </div>;

    }
});
```

 The `replaceState()` method is used when existing values are to be cleared and new ones have to be added.

Here's what the app looks like when it is run for the first time:

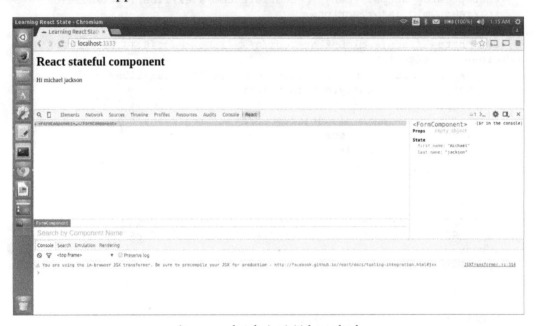

App screenshot during initial page load

After the page initially loads, the value of the `first_name` attribute is `michael`, but when the `onClick` function is called the value changes to `undefined`. The component states with the attributes `first_name` and `last_name` have been replaced with only `last_name` when `replaceState()` is called. The following screenshot illustrates this:

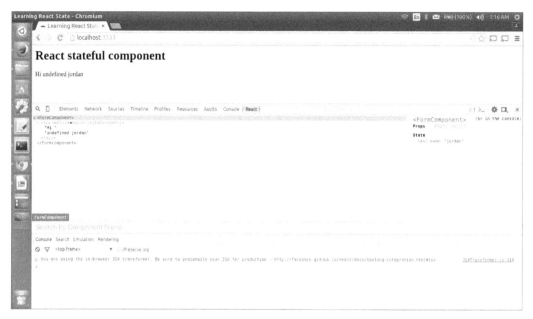

Re-rendering the component after replaceState() is called

A React state example using an interactive form

Let's build a form and see how the values can be passed between Component1 and Component2, as in the next example.

Here's a snippet of code from index.html:

```
<!DOCTYPE html>
<html>
<head>
<script src="https://cdnjs.cloudflare.com/ajax/libs/react/0.14.0-
rc1/react.min.js"></script>
<script src="https://cdnjs.cloudflare.com/ajax/libs/react/0.13.3/
JSXTransf
ormer.js"></script>
    <script src="https://cdnjs.cloudflare.com/ajax/libs/
    jquery/2.1.1/jquery.min.js"></script>
  <script
  src="https://cdnjs.cloudflare.com/ajax/libs/react/0.14.0-
  rc1/react-dom.js"></script>
  <meta charset="utf-8">
  <title>My React App</title>
</head>
```

```
<body>
  <div id="myApp"></div>
    <script type="text/jsx", src="react_state.js"></script>
</body>
</html>
```

This code shows how to pass values between components. The next code snippet is in the `react_state.js` file:

```
/* declaration of React component1 with initial values and the
changed value to be set in  the update function.
*/
var Component1 =
React.createClass({
  getInitialState:function(){
    return {
      name: 'hi',
      id: 1
    };
  },
  update: function(e){
    this.setState({name: e.target.value});
  },
  render:function(){
    return (
      <div>
/* The render method returns the Component2 with props name and
the value to be called on update method*/
      < Component2 name={this.state.name} update={this.update}
      />
      </div>
      );


  }
});
/* Declaration of Component2 which calls the update function when
onChange method is called. */
var Component2 = React.createClass({
  render:function(){
    return (
      <div>
        <input type="text" onChange={this.props.update} />
        <br />
        <b>{this.props.name}</b>
      </div>
```

```
    );

  }
});
ReactDOM.render(< Component1 name="this is the text property"  />,
document.getElementById('myApp'));
```

When we first run the code we see:

User interactive form

After typing in the textbox, the value below automatically changes, as seen here:

Form data updated using this.setState()

Let's now dig deeper into how events flow within a React ecosystem.

Events

React uses SyntheticEvent, which is a cross-browser wrapper around the browser's native event. So all the event handlers in the react applications will be passed instances of SyntheticEvent. React's event ecosystem has the same interface as any of the browser's native events with the advantage that it works identically in all the browsers and provides stopPropagation() and preventDefault() too.

If React is installed as an NPM module, then these SyntheticEvent-related files can be found in the following location within your app: app/node_modules/react/lib.

All these events comply with the W3C standard. The main event flow happens as:

- Dispatching the event : @param {object} dispatchConfig
- Marker identifying the event target: @param {object} dispatchMarker
- Native event: @param {object} nativeEvent

The way React uses this event delegation is by listening to the nodes that have listeners. Depending on the event handlers on the particular node, the synthetic event system of React implements its own bubbling.

Some of the event names in the Synthetic Event system are as follows. Refer to the Facebook documentation for the complete list of the listed registered events.

Form events

- Event names for Form events are:

  ○ onChange, onInput, onSubmit

 For more information about the onChange event, refer to Forms (https://facebook.github.io/react/docs/forms.html).

Mouse events

- Event names for Mouse events are:

  ○ onClick, onContextMenu, onDoubleClick, onDrag, onDragEnd, onDragEnter, onDragExit

  ○ onDragLeave, onDragOver, onDragStart, onDrop, onMouseDown, onMouseEnter, onMouseLeave

  ○ onMouseMove, onMouseOut, onMouseOver, onMouseUp

Let's show an example of some of the different events called by the SyntheticEvent system on a React component.

In the JavaScript file, we have the following code snippet:

```
/* React component EventBox is decalred which shows the different
functions it fires in response of diffenrent Synthetic events.*/
var EventBox = React.createClass({

  getInitialState:function(){
    return {e: 'On initial page load'}
  },

  update: function(e){
    this.setState({e: e.type})
  },

  render:function(){
    return (
      <div>
        <textarea
/*Following are the various events (on the left hand side ). In
response of all these events then the update function is called.
*/
          onKeyDown={this.update}
          onKeyPress={this.update}
          onCopy={this.update}
          onFocus={this.update}
          onBlur={this.update}
          onDoubleClick={this.update}
/>
        <h1>{this.state.e}</h1>
      </div>
    );});
```

The following code displays a textbox in the browser. As we type in the box, the corresponding event type prints out below. Since we are updating the state with `event.type`, the corresponding event is shown below as we type in the box.

```
ReactDOM.render(<EventBox />,
document.getElementById('myTextarea'));
```

User interactive form

nativeEvent

Sometimes we may need the underlying browser event for our application; in that case, we need to use its `nativeEvent` attribute. This code shows how we can attach DOM events, which are not provided by the React synthetic event system, to a React component.

The following is the code snippet for the `index.js` file:

```
/* React component MyBrowserDimension, with nativeEvent attribute
which is needed for manipulating the underlying browser
events(window.innerWidth, window.innerHeight). */
var MyBrowserDimension = React.createClass({
getInitialState:function(){
    return {
      width: window.innerWidth,
      height: window.innerHeight
    };
  },
```

```
update: function(){
    this.setState({
        height: window.innerHeight,
        width: window.innerWidth
    });
},
```

//componentDidMount is called after the component is mounted and //
has a DOM presentation. This is often a place where we will //attach
generic DOM events.

```
componentDidMount:function(){
    window.addEventListener('resize', this.update );
    window.addEventListener('resize', this.update );
},

componentWillUnmount:function(){
    window.removeEventListener('resize', this.update );
    window.removeEventListener('resize', this.update );
},

render:function(){
    return <div>
        <p>My Browser Window current Inner Width is:
        {this.state.width} pixels</p>
        <p>My Browser Window current height is {this.state.height}
        pixels</p>
    </div>;
}
});

ReactDOM.render(<MyBrowserDimension />,
document.getElementById('myApp'));
```

Here's the source code for the corresponding HTML page:

```
<!DOCTYPE html>
<html>
<head>
<script src="https://cdnjs.cloudflare.com/ajax/libs/react/0.14.0-
rc1/react.js"></script>
<script src="https://cdnjs.cloudflare.com/ajax/libs/react/0.14.0-
rc1/react-dom.js"></script>
<script
src="https://cdnjs.cloudflare.com/ajax/libs/react/0.13.3/JSXTransf
ormer.js"></script>
```

```
      <meta charset="utf-8">
      <title>React DOM attributes</title>
   </head>
   <body>
   <div id="myApp"></div>
       <script type="text/jsx", src="index.js"></script>
   </html>
```

From the following screenshots, we can see that as we resize the browser window, the width and height values change. The first image shows the full size [1311/681] of the browser.

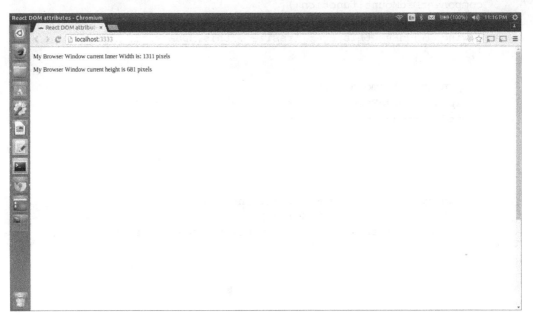

App showing browser's native attributes

The second image from the preceding application code shows that after resizing the browser window, the pixel values changed to 497/219.

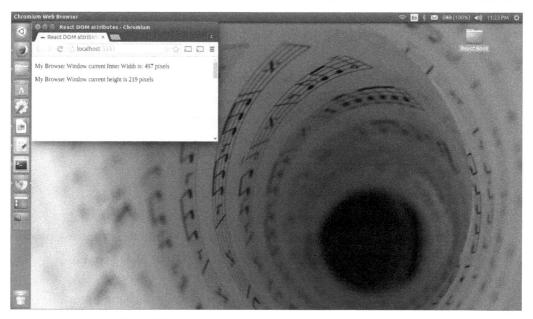

Native DOM attributes changing with browser window changes

According to the Facebook developer team (`http://facebook.github.io/react/tips/dom-event-listeners.html`):

> *"The event callbacks which are declared in a React app, are all bound to the React components. These event callbacks are not tied to the original elements. By autobinding, these methods are automatically bounded to the current element."*

Also, every `SyntheticEvent` object has the following attributes:

- `boolean bubbles`: All event handlers are triggered in the event bubbling phases; it can be `true`/`false`

- `boolean cancelable`: Whether the SyntheticEvent object can be cancelled or not (true/false)

- `DOMEventTarget currentTarget`: As per W3C recommendations, the `currentTarget` event property returns the element whose event listeners triggered the event

This is particularly useful during capturing and bubbling.

The `currentTarget` property always refers to the element whose event listener triggered the event, as opposed to the `target` property, which returns the element that triggered the event.

- `boolean defaultPrevented`: Whether the `SyntheticEvent` object can be prevented by default or not (true/false)

- `number eventPhase`: The `eventPhase` event property returns a number that indicates which phase of the event flow is currently being evaluated (see: `https://developer.mozilla.org/en-US/docs/Web/API/Event/eventPhase`)

  The number is represented by four constants:

  > `0` – `NONE`.

  > `1` – `CAPTURING_PHASE`: The event flow is within the capturing phase.

  > `2` – `AT_TARGET`: The event flow is in the target phase, that is, it is being evaluated at the event target.

  > `3` – `BUBBLING_PHASE`: The event flow is in the bubbling phase.

- `boolean isTrusted`: As per JS recommendations, in Chrome, Firefox, and Opera, the event is trusted (returns true) if it is invoked by the user, and not trusted if it is invoked by a script ((returns false)).

- `DOMEvent nativeEvent`: `nativeEvent` is a kind of `DOMEvent`.

- `void preventDefault()`: The `preventDefault()` method does cancel the event if it is cancellable (it cancels the default action of the method) but it does not prevent further propagation of an event through the DOM. The return type of `preventDefault()` in React is void.

- `void stopPropagation()`: `stopPropagation` is called to prevent events from bubbling up to their parent elements, which thereby prevents any parent event handlers from being invoked.

- `boolean isDefaultPrevented()`: `isDefaultPrevented` is used to check whether the `preventDefault()` method is called (true) or not (false).

- `boolean isPropagationStopped()`: `isPropagationStopped` is used to check whether the `stopPropagation()` method is called (true) or not (false).

- `DOMEventTarget target`: It is used to identify the target of the `SyntheticEvent` object declared, which returns the element that triggered the event. The return type is in `DOMEventTarget`.

- `number timeStamp`: This is used to identify the timestamp of the `SyntheticEvent` object declared. The return type is in the form number.

- `string type`: This is used to identify a kind of `SyntheticEvent` object declared. The return type is in the form string.

Note: As of v0.14, returning false from an event handler will no longer stop event propagation. Instead, `e.stopPropagation()` or `e.preventDefault()` should be triggered manually, as appropriate.

Event pooling

A **pool** is a place where events/objects are kept, so that they can be reused at a later stage, after being garbage collected. In the React ecosystem, the event objects (`SyntheticEvent`) that are received in callbacks are pooled. As mentioned before, after the event callback has been called, `SyntheticEvent` will be put back in the pool with empty attributes, which thereby reduces the pressure on the Garbage Collector. Next are some key highlights for event pooling as mentioned in the Facebook documentation as well.

The `SyntheticEvent` system in React is pooled.

> *"This means that the `SyntheticEvent` object will be reused.*
>
> *All properties will be nullified after the event callback has been invoked.*
>
> *This is for performance reasons.*
>
> *We cannot access the event in an asynchronous way.*
>
> *In order to access the event properties in an asynchronous way, we should call* `event.persist()` *on the event, which will remove the synthetic event from the pool and allow references to the event to be retained by user code."*

Supported events

React normalizes events so that they have consistent properties across different browsers.

According to the Facebook documentation (`http://facebook.github.io/react/docs/events.html`)

> *"The event handlers of the Synthetic Events of the React ecosystem are triggered by an event in the bubbling phase."*

Now that we have covered what a state is in the React component and how event handling happens, let's see how we can use these in the app that we were building in the last chapter.

Until the last chapter, we were able to display the likes of a user, using the Graph-API and Facebook login into our app. Based on its props, each component has rendered itself once. Props are immutable: they are passed from the parent and are *owned* by the parent. Now, we will be able to update the name of the liked component onClick on any part of the particular div where the React component resides.

The index.html code snippet for the following example is:

```html
<html>
  <head>
    <title>Learning React State</title>
    <script src="http://fb.me/react-0.13.3.js"></script>
    <script src="http://fb.me/JSXTransformer-0.13.3.js"></script>
  </head>
  <body>
    <h1>Facebook User's list of likes</h1>
    <div id="user"></div>
    <div id="main"></div>
    <a onClick='logout()' href='#'>Logout</a>
    <script>
      window.fbAsyncInit = function() {
        FB.init({
          appId      : '1512084142440038',
          xfbml      : true,
          version    : 'v2.2'
        });

        checkLoginStatusAndLoadUserLikes();
      };

      (function(d, s, id){
         var js, fjs = d.getElementsByTagName(s)[0];
         if (d.getElementById(id)) {return;}
         js = d.createElement(s); js.id = id;
         js.src = "//connect.facebook.net/en_US/sdk/debug.js";
         fjs.parentNode.insertBefore(js, fjs);
       }(document, 'script', 'facebook-jssdk'));
    </script>

    <script type="text/jsx" src="index.js"></script>
  </body>
</html>
```

The following code is within the `js` file:

```
// The following code block explains in order to login to user's
Facebook //account and call the function internally(
loginAndLoadUserLikes) if //successfully connected.
function checkLoginStatusAndLoadUserLikes() {
  FB.getLoginStatus(function(response) {
    if (response.status === 'connected') {
      loadUserAndLikes();
    } else {
      loginAndLoadUserLikes();
    }
  });
}


function loginAndLoadUserLikes() {
  FB.login(function(response) {
    loadUserAndLikes();
  }, {scope: 'user_likes'});
}


//Once logged in, this method should load the details of the
specific user.
var UserDetails = React.createClass({
  render: function () {
    return (
      <section id="user-details">
        <a href={this.props.userDetails.link} target="_blank">
          {this.props.userDetails.name}
        </a>
        {' | '}
        <a href="#" onClick={this.handleLogout}>Logout</a>
      </section>
    )
  },


//Specified user should be able to logout from the respective
account
handleLogout: function () {
    FB.logout(function () {
      alert("You're logged out, refresh the page in order to login
      again.");
    });
  }
});
```

```
//Once logged in, this method should load the likes pages of the
specific user.
function loadUserAndLikes () {
  FB.api('/me', function (userResponse) {
    React.render(<UserDetails userDetails={userResponse} />,
    document.getElementById('user'));

    var fields = { fields: 'category,name,picture.type(normal)' };
    FB.api('/me/likes', fields, function (likesResponse) {
      React.render(<UserLikesList list={likesResponse.data} />,
      document.getElementById('main'));
    });
  });
}


//Once logged in, this method should list the liked pages of the
specific user.
var UserLikesList = React.createClass({
  render: function() {
    var items = this.props.list.map(function (likeObject) {
      return <UserLikeItem data={likeObject} />;
    });

    return (
      <ul id="user-likes-list">
        {items}
      </ul>
    );
  }
});
var UserLikeItem = React.createClass({
  getInitialState: function() {
    return {data_name: this.props.data.name};
  },
  handleClick: function(){
    this.setState({
  data_name: 'I liked it'})
    },
```

```
  render: function() {
    var props_data = this.props.data;

    return (
      <div onClick={this.handleClick}>
        <img src={props_data.picture.data.url}
        title={props_data.name} />
        <h1> {this.state.data_name}  <small>{props_data.category}</
small></h1>
      </div>
    );
  }
});
```

The highlighted part shows the changes we made, in order to save the state.

- getInitialState(): is declared by initializing the value of the liked data name's value from the props data. getInitialState() executes exactly once during the lifecycle of the component and sets up the initial state of the component.

The reason for the *mutable state* (the state that can be changed) is as follows:

- The **mutable state** is introduced to the component (UserLikedItem). In order to implement interactions, this.state can be changed by calling this.setState() and is private to the component. When the state updates, the component (UserLikedItem) re-renders itself.

- render() methods are written by the Facebook developer team, declaratively as functions of this.props and this.state. They ensure that the framework guarantees the UI is always consistent with the inputs.

- This is a perfect example of how data flows between components in the React ecosystem. The property (data) is passed from the React component `UserLikesList` to another component, `UserLikedItem`.

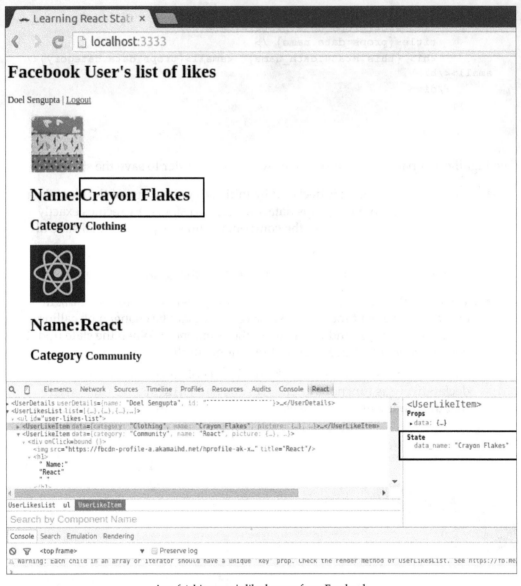

App fetching user's liked pages from Facebook

React attaches event handlers to components using a camelCase naming convention. We attach an `onClick` handler to the `div` element, so that whenever a user clicks at any portion of the image or the image name or category, it will change to **I liked it**.

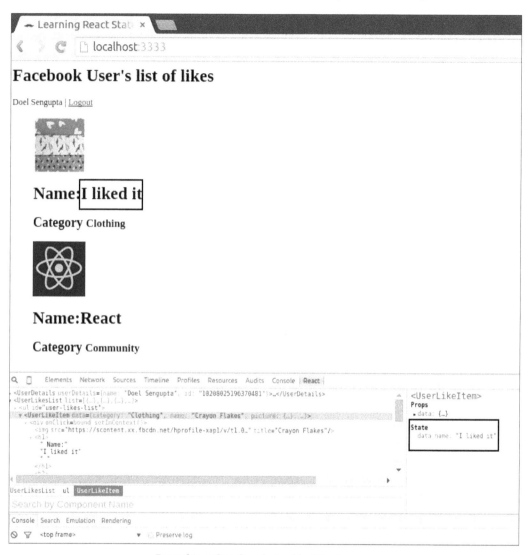

React this.setState() replacing liked item's name

Summary

According to Facebook's Reconciliation documentation (`https://facebook.github.io/react/docs/reconciliation.html`)

> *"React's key design decision is to make the API seem like it re-renders the whole app on every update."*

Thus, whenever the `setState()` method is called on an object, that particular node is marked. At the end of the event loop, all the nodes are re-rendered where the `setState()` method is called.

React is fast because it never talks to the DOM directly. It maintains an in-memory representation of the actual DOM. Whenever the `render()` method is called, it returns a mapping of the actual DOM. React can detect (using a diff algorithm) changes in the mapped DOM compared to the in-memory representation. It then re-renders the changes and updates the UI likewise.

The event ecosystem in React is implemented by a full synthetic event system (`SyntheticEvent()`). Cross-browser efficiency is achieved as all the events bubble up consistently.

In the current chapter, we have explored the stateful components in React and how the synthetic event system is handled in React applications. States are used for those properties in React components that are mutable. In the next chapter, we will explore the component lifecycle and how these lifecycle methods interact with various events and the DOM as a whole.

5
Component Life cycle and Newer ECMAScript in React

So far, we have explored React component properties and how we need to initialize, update, and change the component's state(s) for interactive applications. Let's now explore the lifecycle of such a React component in this chapter. We will also dig into future ECMAScript syntax and a few changes that the React community also used from version 0.13.0. For this, we will review some ES6 and ES7 features within the React library.

While creating any React component by calling `React.createClass()`, we need to always have a render method. This render method returns a description of the DOM. React has a performance edge in our applications because React maintains a fast in-memory representation of the DOM and never directly interacts with the actual DOM. Thus, when the render method returns the description of the DOM, React can compare the difference between the actual DOM and the in-memory representation, and, based on the difference(s), re-renders the view accordingly.

In this chapter, we will cover the following topics:

- React component lifecycle
- Using React with ECMAScript

React component lifecycle

As per Facebook's React documentation from `http://facebook.github.io/react/docs/working-with-the-browser.html`, the React component lifecycle can be broadly classified into three categories as follows:

> "**Mounting**: *A component is being inserted into the DOM.*
>
> **Updating**: *A component is being re-rendered to determine if the DOM should be updated.*
>
> **Unmounting**: *A component is being removed from the DOM.*"

React provides lifecycle methods that you can specify to hook into this process. We provide `will` methods, which are called right before something happens, and `did` methods which are called right after something happens.

Mounting category

Mounting is the process of publishing the virtual representation of a component into the final UI representation (for example, DOM or native components). In a browser, it would mean publishing a React element into an actual DOM element in the DOM tree.

Method Name	Method Function
`getInitialState()`	This method is invoked before the component is mounted. In the case of stateful components, this method returns the initial state data.
`componentWillMount()`	This method is called just before React mounts the component in the DOM.
`componentDidMount()`	This method is called immediately after mounting occurs. The initialization process that DOM nodes requires should go within this method.

Like in the previous chapters, most of the code in the `index.html` is the same. We will only be replacing the contents of the JavaScript file.

The code of `index.html` will become as follows:

```
<!DOCTYPE html>
<html>
<head>
<script src="https://cdnjs.cloudflare.com/ajax/libs/react/0.14.0-
rc1/react.min.js"></script>
```

```
<script src="https://cdnjs.cloudflare.com/ajax/
libs/react/0.13.3/JSXTransformer.js"></script>
    <script src="https://cdnjs.cloudflare.com/
    ajax/libs/react/0.14.0-rc1/react-dom.js"></script>
    <meta charset="utf-8">
    <title>My React App</title>
</head>
<body>
    <div id="app"></div>
        <script type="text/jsx", src="index.js"></script>
</body>
</html>
```

Let's illustrate the lifecycle method, using a code snippet. Place the following code in the index.js file:

```
var MyButton = React.createClass({
        getInitialState: function(){
            return {value: 11}
        },
        addOnClick: function(){
            this.setState({value: this.state.value +  2});
        },
        render: function(){
            console.log("myButton React component is rendering");
            return <button
            onClick={this.addOnClick}>{this.state.value}</button>
            }
});
ReactDOM.render(<MyButton />,
document.getElementById('myComponent'));
```

Initially, we can see the value of myButton set to **11**:

The value of `myButton` increases by two when the `onClick(addOnClick)` event occurs. Thus, the value of state changes.

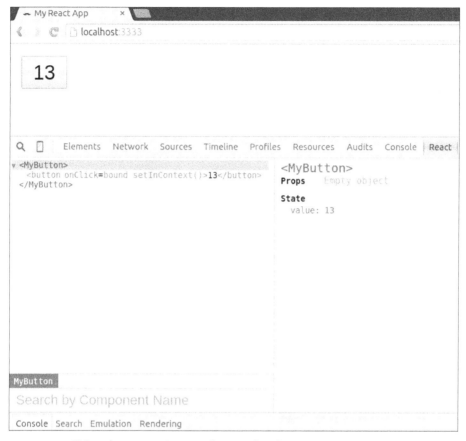

Value of `myButton` increases by two when the `onClick` event occurs

If we add the `componentWillMount` method to the preceding code, we will be able to see that the React component is only mounted in the DOM once, but is rendered each time we click on the button.

```
componentWillMount: function(){
console.log('MyButton component is mounting');
},
```

The screenshot of the app component mounting on the DOM shows in the console, **MyButton component is mounting**.

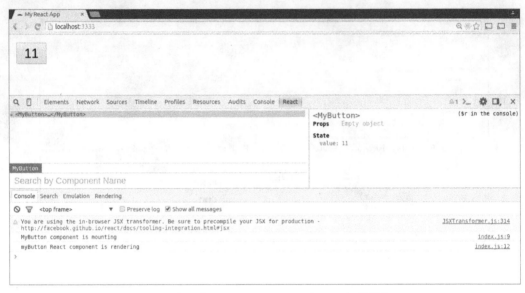

Screenshot of app component mounting on the DOM

Let's implement the last mounting method, `componentDidMount`, which is called after the component is mounted. As you can see in the next screenshot, the console shows the component has been mounted once but the component is rendered the number of times we click on the button, four times in this case: `11 + (2*4) =19`.

```
componentDidMount: function(){
console.log('MyButton component is mounted');
},
```

The screenshot shows methods where mounting and mounted on the DOM is called once, though rendering happens. Thus, after the `componentDidMount` method is executed, in the console we can see the output **MyButton component is mounted**.

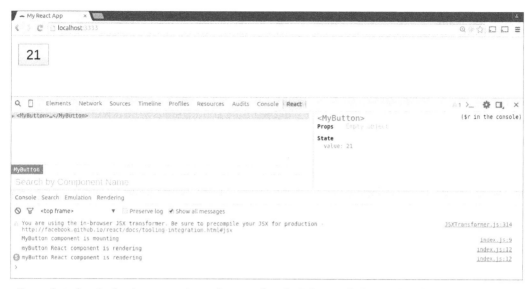

Screenshot of methods where mounting and mounted on the DOM is called once, though rendering happens

Updating category

The React component lifecycle allows updating components at runtime. This can be done using the following methods:

Method Name	Method Function
componentWillReceiveProps(ob ject nextProps)	This method is invoked when a mounted React component receives new properties (props). This means you can use it to compare between this.props, the current set of properties, and nextProps, the new property values. There is no similar method like componentWillReceiveState. Thus, an incoming property transition may cause a state change, but an incoming state may not cause a property change. If we want to perform some operation in response to a state change, we would need to use the method componentWillUpdate.

Thus, the component's property changes will be rendered in the updated view without re-rendering the view. |

Method Name	Method Function
shouldComponentUpdate(object nextProps, object nextState)	This method is invoked when a component requires an update in the DOM. The return type is boolean (true/false). It returns false when there is no change in the props and/or state, which will prevent componentWillUpdate and componentDidUpdate from being called.
componentWillUpdate(object nextProps, object nextState)	As the name suggests, this method is invoked immediately before updating occurs, but not in the first render call. this.setState() cannot be called within this lifecycle method. To update a state in response to a property change, use componentWillReceiveProps instead.
componentDidUpdate(object prevProps, object prevState)	This is invoked immediately after updating occurs in the DOM and not during the initial render() call.

Let's add the preceding methods in our code:

```
//Updating lifecycle methods
        shouldComponentUpdate: function() {
        console.log('ShouldComponentUpdate');
            return true;
          },
        componentWillReceiveProps: function(nextProps) {
            console.log('ComponentWillRecieveProps invoked');
          },
        componentWillUpdate: function() {
            console.log('ComponentWillUpdate invoked');
        },
        componentDidUpdate: function() {
            console.log('ComponentDidUpdate invoked');
        },
```

Execute the preceding code to see the following output. We can see the various lifecycle events of the React component and the corresponding output they give in the console.

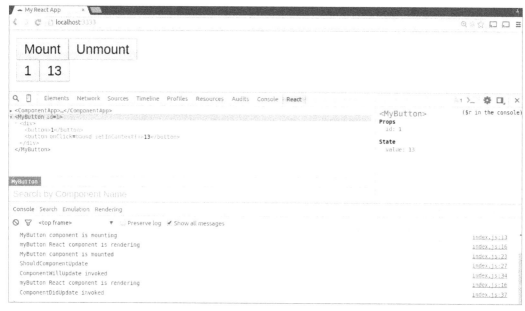

Screenshot of component being updated

Unmounting category

componentWillUnmount() is invoked immediately before a component is unmounted and destroyed. You should perform any necessary cleanup here.

```
componentWillUnmount: function(){
console.log('Umounting MyButton component');
}
```

Here's the complete example encompassing all the lifecycle methods of a React component. The index.html is the same as the preceding.

The code of index.html:

```
<!DOCTYPE html>
<html>
<head>
<script src="https://cdnjs.cloudflare.com/ajax/libs/react/0.14.0-rc1/
react.min.js"></script>
<script src="https://cdnjs.cloudflare.com/
ajax/libs/react/0.13.3/JSXTransformer.js"></script>
```

```
    <script src="https://cdnjs.cloudflare.com/
    ajax/libs/react/0.14.0-rc1/react-dom.js"></script>
    <meta charset="utf-8">
    <title>My React App</title>
</head>
<body>
    <div id="app"></div>
        <script type="text/jsx", src="index.js"></script>
</body>
</html>
```

Here is the corresponding `index.js` code:

```
var MyButton = React.createClass({
    getDefaultProps: function() {
        console.log('GetDefaultProps is invoked');
        return {id: 1};
    },
    getInitialState: function(){
        return {value: 11}
    },
    addOnClick: function(){
        this.setState({value: this.state.value +  2});
    },
    componentWillMount: function(){
        console.log('MyButton component is mounting');
    },
    render: function(){
        console.log("myButton React component is rendering");
        return ( <div>
        <button>{this.props.id}</button>
        <button
        onClick={this.addOnClick}>{this.state.value}</button>
        </div>);
        },
        componentDidMount: function(){
        console.log('MyButton component is mounted');
        },

//Updating lifecycle methods
    shouldComponentUpdate: function() {
        console.log('ShouldComponentUpdate');
        return true;
    },
```

```
    componentWillReceiveProps: function(nextProps) {
        console.log('ComponentWillRecieveProps invoked');
    },
    componentWillUpdate: function() {
        console.log('ComponentWillUpdate invoked');
    },
    componentDidUpdate: function() {
        console.log('ComponentDidUpdate invoked');
    },

//Unmounting Lifecycle Methods
    componentWillUnmount: function(){
        console.log('Umounting MyButton component');
    }

});

var ComponentApp = React.createClass({
    mount: function(){
        ReactDOM.render(<MyButton />,
        document.getElementById('myApp'));
    },
    unmount: function(){
        ReactDOM.unmountComponentAtNode(document.getElementById
        ('myApp'));
    },
    render: function(){
        return (
        <div>
        <button onClick={this.mount}>Mount</button>
        <button onClick={this.unmount}>Unmount</button>
        <div id="myApp"></div>
        </div>
        );
    }
});

ReactDOM.render(<ComponentApp />, document.getElementById('app'));
```

Observe the following:

- After executing the preceding code, we will be able to see two buttons as **Mount** and **Unmount**
- The initial value of the component is set to **11**
- `onClick` on the React component; its value is increased by a value of two
- While clicking on the **Mount**, the lifecycle methods of the React component is called
- For each of these lifecycle methods, we can see an output in the console

Screenshot of unmouting the component from the DOM

Note: Mounted composite components support the method `component.forceUpdate()`. This method can be invoked on any mounted component, in case of some changes in the deeper aspect of the component, without using `this.setState()`.

Our React component's lifecycles are shown next. The lifecycles are highlighted in the right portion of the developer tool:

Screenshot showing the React component's lifecycle, as highlighted in the right portion of the developer tool

Other ES (ECMAScript) versions in React

In the second half of this chapter, we will explore how React supports newer versions of ECMAScript. Until now, we have explored the different lifecycle methods in a React component. In this section of the chapter, we will dig into something different: how changes in the new version of ECMAScript have been adopted by React.

ES6

ES6 is the current version of the ECMAScript Language Specification Standard. Further details about the changes and the new things incorporated can be found on the Mozilla Development Network site: `https://developer.mozilla.org/en-US/docs/Web/JavaScript/New_in_JavaScript/ECMAScript_6_support_in_Mozilla`

Complete documentation for ES6 is beyond the scope of this book.

According to the Facebook documentation:

Starting with React 0.13.0 a transpiler allows us to use ES6 classes. JavaScript originally didn't have a built-in class system. The developer team wanted class creation using the idiomatic JavaScript style. Therefore instead of `React.createClass` the developer team has introduced a component. You can use the transpiler they ship with `react-tools` by making use of the harmony option and setting it to `true` as follows:

```
jsx -harmony
```

By looking through `https://www.npmjs.com/package/react-tools`, you can find details of the different options you can pass with the JSX Transformer. `--harmony` turns on JS transformations such as ES6 classes and so on.

Thus, ES6 syntax will be transformed into ES5 compatible syntaxes.

> **Transpiling** is a method for taking source code written in one language and transforming it into another language that has a similar level of abstraction.
>
> When TypeScript is compiled and is transformed by the compiler into JavaScript, it has very similar levels of abstraction. Hence, it is called transpiling.

Here, React classes are defined as a plain JavaScript class. Let's go through the following code from their documentation with some modifications and explanations.

Code within `index.html`:

```html
<!DOCTYPE html>
<html>
<head>
<script src="https://cdnjs.cloudflare.com/ajax/libs/react/0.14.0-rc1/
react.js"></script>
<script src="https://cdnjs.cloudflare.com/ajax/libs/react/0.14.0-rc1/
react-dom.js"></script>
<script src="https://cdnjs.cloudflare.com/ajax
/libs/react/0.13.3/JSXTransformer.js"></script>
  <meta charset="utf-8">
  <title>React ES6</title>
  <h1>ok</h1>
  </style>
</head>
<body>
<div id="react-content"></div>
    <script type="text/jsx;harmony=true" src="index.js"></script>
</html>
```

The highlighted line with the argument as `harmony=true` ensures that the jsx syntax with ES6 code should be transpiled into JavaScript using ES5 syntax.

Code within `index.js`:

```
//line 1
class Es6Component extends React.Component {

//line 2
render() {

  return <div onClick={this._handleClick}>
  Hi There, I am learning ES6 in React.</div>;

}

_handleClick() {

  console.log("hi");

}

}

ReactDOM.render(<Es6Component />, document.getElementById('react-
content '));
```

Explanation:

- Line 1: Declaring the React component `Es6Component`, which extends from `React.Component` instead of `React.createClass`
- Line 2: The render function call syntax is different. Before, it was
  `render: function()`

Here is a screenshot demonstrating it:

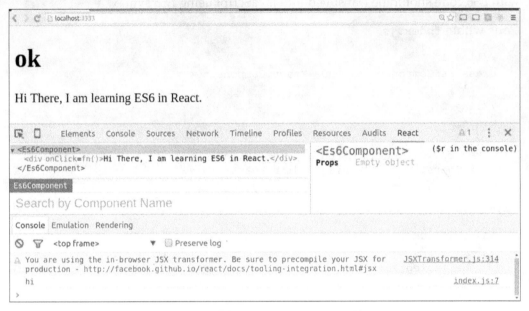

Screenshot of the React component using ES6

Instead of `getInitialState` in `React.createClass`, using ES6 the new constructor has the new own state property in `React.Component`, which is exported.

```
export class Counter extends React.Component

/* The constructor of the newly created React class, Counter.
There are the following things to be noted:
call to super(props)And instead of calling getInitialState()
ifecycle method, React team used the instance property called
this.state() */

constructor(props) {super(props);
    this.state = {count: props.initialCount};
  }

  tick() {
    this.setState({count: this.state.count + 1});
  }

  render() {
    return (
      <div onClick={this.tick.bind(this)}>
        Clicks: {this.state.count}
```

```
      </div>
    );
  }
}
```

/* For validation and default values purposes propTypes and
defaultProps are inbuilt within React's component. Here the
propTypes and defaultProps are defined as properties on the
constructor instead within the the class body. */

// Declares the React's class Counter property types as number
Counter.propTypes = { initialCount: React.PropTypes.number };

/* sets the defaultProps for the Counter React class as
initialCount being 0. These values are passed as super(props)*/
Counter.defaultProps = { initialCount: 0 };

Screenshot of the React component using ES6

Another feature of React using ES6 is No Autobinding.

As with ES6 classes, which do not automatically bind to the instance, we need to use bind.(this) **OR** use the arrow sign (=>) explicitly in ES6.

Following these ES6 syntaxes, we can rewrite our sample app from Chapter XX, which lists the user's likes in Facebook. Just as before, if the user clicks on the liked-page name, the string **I Liked it** will be updated on the page.

The changes as per the new ES6 syntaxes are highlighted next:

```
use 'strict';
function checkLoginStatusAndLoadUserLikes() {

  FB.getLoginStatus(function(response) {
    if (response.status === 'connected') {
      loadUserAndLikes();
    } else {
      loginAndLoadUserLikes();
    }
  });
}

function loginAndLoadUserLikes() {
  FB.login(function(response) {
    loadUserAndLikes();
  }, {scope: 'user_likes'});
}

//var UserDetails = React.createClass({

class UserDetails extends React.component {
  render() {
    return (
      <section id="user-details">
        <a href={this.props.userDetails.link} target="__blank">
          {this.props.userDetails.name}
        </a>
        {' | '}
        <a href="#" onClick={this.handleLogout}>Logout</a>
      </section>
    )
  },

  handleLogout: function () {
    FB.logout(function () {
      alert("You're logged out, refresh the page in order to login
again.");
    });
  }
```

```
});

function loadUserAndLikes () {
  FB.api('/me', function (userResponse) {
    ReactDOM.render(<UserDetails userDetails={userResponse} />,
    document.getElementById('user'));

    var fields = { fields: 'category,name,picture.type(normal)' };
    FB.api('/me/likes', fields, function (likesResponse) {
      React.render(<UserLikesList list={likesResponse.data} />,
      document.getElementById('main'));
    });
  });
}

//var UserLikesList = React.createClass({
class UserLikesList extends React.Component {
  render() {
    let items = this.props.list.map(function (likeObject) {
      return <UserLikeItem data={likeObject} />;
    });

    return (
      <ul id="user-likes-list">
        {items}
      </ul>
    );
  }
//});

}

//var UserLikeItem = React.createClass({

class UserLikeItem extends React.createComponent {

 //getInitialState: function() {
   // return {data_name: this.props.data.name};
 //},
  handleClick(){
     this.setState({
    data_name: 'I liked it'})
    },

  render() {
    let props_data = this.props.data;
```

```
    return (
      <div onClick={this.handleClick}>
        <img src={props_data.picture.data.url}
        title={props_data.name} />

        <h1> Name:{this.state.data_name} </h1>
    <h2>Category <small>{props_data.category}</small></h2>
      </div>
    );
  }
}
```

  `let` is used instead of `var` to declare a variable in a local scope.

The output remains the same, as per the next screenshot:

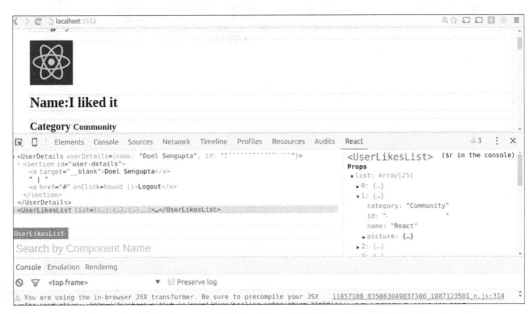

Screenshot of the React app, fetching the user's liked pages, using ES6 syntaxes

  Note: ES6 does not support mixins. Mixins will be covered later in this book in *Chapter 7, Making your Component Reusable*, in more detail. Mixins are used to write reusable codes in React applications.

ES7

ECMAScript7 is one step beyond ES6. Even before ES6 was finalized, new features started to be proposed. Please view the experimental and stabilized feature list at the following URL:

```
https://developer.mozilla.org/en-US/docs/Web/JavaScript/New_in_
JavaScript/ECMAScript_7_support_in_Mozilla
```

Keeping ES7 in mind, the React developer community presented us with some syntactic sugar to the existing React class code. In the future version of JavaScript (ES7), there can be more declarative syntax for property initialization, as this would be a more idiomatic way of expressing. Here's a quick example:

```
// Future Version
export class Counter extends React.Component {
  static propTypes = { initialCount: React.PropTypes.number };
  static defaultProps = { initialCount: 0 };
  state = { count: this.props.initialCount };
  //constructor
// render method
    );
  }
}
```

Summary

In this chapter, we have gone through the lifecycle of a typical React component, the various phases it undergoes, and how React renders the view based on the diff-ing algorithm (that is, calculating the deltas between the virtual DOM and the actual DOM).

In the second part of the chapter, we explored the future of ECMAScript and how React.js already supports it. For this, we have used sample code examples from Facebook's documentation.

In the next chapter, we will discuss React's reusable components known as mixins. We will also explore how we can add validations in a React-based application. Validations are required for apps that accept user input. User inputs should be validated before being sent to the server, to prevent malicious or invalid content from being sent.

6
Reacting with Flux

So far in the previous chapters, we have dug deep into the react world. Let's now explore the new dimension of react world, Flux, which is nothing but a unidirectional dataflow architecture. Flux is developed by the Facebook internal development team and is used in order to build client-side web applications at Facebook.

We will cover the following topics as we go along:

- The synopsis of Flux versus the MVC architecture
- Actions
- Dispatchers
- Stores
- Controller-Views and Views

An overview of Flux

Flux should not be confused as a framework based on ReactJS. Flux is an architecture and is designed in order to reduce the complexity of a huge application built with **Model View Controller** (**MVC**) architecture and has been designed as an alternative of MVC.

The following are the different Flux components:

- View – This is like for any web app, the views (basically the react component) receives the event and passes it to the Actions
- Action – They are helper methods (`actionCreators`) that pass the data (payload) and `actionType`, received from an external API/view to a dispatcher

- Dispatcher—These are Central hub of all registered callbacks. It receives the actions and acts as a "traffic controller" before it passes it to the Stores

- Store—It is a data layer that stores all the computations and business logic. It is also responsible for storing the application state and the single source of truth for the application state. It receives the action from the dispatchers based on the registered callbacks.

- Controller-View—This receives the state from the stores based on the `changeEvents` and passes it to the React views component via props.

A diagram here illustrates this:

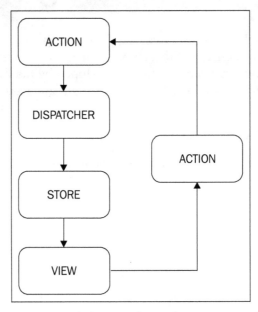

Typical Flux Data Flow Architecture

Flux versus the MVC architecture

In a typical application built on the MVC architecture, the views get updated from the data, which is typically stored in the models. As the application grows, the number of models and views also grow, and there grows the interdependency among the various models. Therefore the views also get tdependent on multiple models, thus increasing the complexity of the application.

The interdependence of views and models can create diffraction in the source of truth, leading to increased application complexity and unpredictability. As a result, there needs to be a solution to internalize the control by moving all the control into the individual pieces.

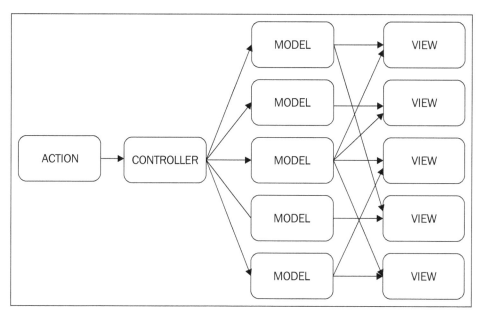

Issue with a growing app built with MVC

Flux advantages

According to the Facebook Flux development team, the objects within a Flux application are highly decoupled, and adhere very strongly to the first part of the Law of Demeter: the principle that each object within a system should know as little as possible about the other objects in the system. This results in software that is more.

- Maintainable
- Adaptable
- Testable
- Easier and more predictable for new engineering team members to understand

The following is a Flux application structure of our `library_app` application.

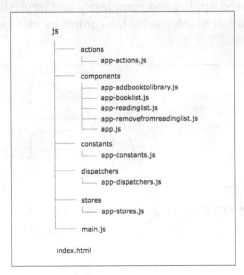

Our Library App Structure

Flux components

Let's dive into an application, built with Flux architecture with React View. Here, we will be building an app named `library_app`. This is a basic Flux-based ReactJS app, where we can borrow books from the `library_app` store to our reading list. Once we finish the book, we can strike it off from our reading list.

From the command line execute:

`sudo npm install flux`

The above will install the flux package as a node module and your library_app application will have a directory called node_modules with the flux library installed within it.

Actions

Actions are typically the data that enters into an application, either directly from the View or from an external Web API. Each action is nothing but a JavaScript method, which contains two parts: the `actionType` and the actual data. The `actionCreators` methods are simply discrete, semantic helper functions that facilitate passing data to the *dispatcher* in the form of an *action*. The different types of actions are declared as a JavaScript object, in a file named `App-Constants.js`. According to the Flux app hierarchy, the `App-Contstants.js` file resides under `src/js/constants`. Typical example for such a file looks like the following:

```
module.exports = {
        ADD_BOOK: 'ADD_BOOK',
        DELETE_BOOK: 'DELETE_BOOK',
        INC_BOOK_COUNT: 'INC_BOOK_COUNT',
        DEC_BOOK_COUNT: 'DEC_BOOK_COUNT'
}
```

Here, `ADD_BOOK`, `DELETE_BOOK` are the actions.

 Actions, by itself, do not contain any functionality of their own. Actions are typically executed by the stores and are available in order to trigger the views. In React, we have handful of helper methods named `actionCreators`, which ideally creates the action object and passes the action to the Flux dispatcher (`AppDispatcher`).

All the actions defined in the `AppConstants` are declared in the `AppActions`.

The use of constants in the `AppConstants`, which declares the action names, helps the developer to understand the app's functionality. As in our case, it deals with books.

In the following example while adding books in a `library_app` store, we are dealing with four `actionTypes`:

- ADD_BOOK
- DELETE_BOOK
- INC_BOOK_COUNT
- DEC_BOOK_COUNT

The actions (such as `addBook`, `removeBook`, `incBookCount`, and `decBookCount`) are unique based on their `actionType` attribute. Thus, when these actions are dispatched by the dispatchers to the stores, stores mutates themselves depending on the specific callback registered with the dispatchers.

Typical action file resides in `library_app/src/js/actions/app-actions.js`:

```
var AppConstants = require('../constants/app-constants');
var AppDispatcher = require('../dispatchers/app-dispatchers');

var AppActions = {
  addBook:function(item){
        AppDispatcher.handleViewAction({
          actionType: AppConstants.ADD_BOOK,
          item: item
```

```
        })
    },
    removeBook:function(index){
        AppDispatcher.handleViewAction({
            actionType: AppConstants.REMOVE_BOOK,
            index: index
        })
    },
    incBookCount:function(index){
        AppDispatcher.handleViewAction({
            actionType: AppConstants.INC_BOOK_COUNT,
            item: index
        })
    },
    decBookCount:function(index){
        AppDispatcher.handleViewAction({
            actionType: AppConstants.DEC_BOOK_COUNT,
            item: index
        })
    }
}

module.exports =  AppActions;
```

Dispatchers

As the name aptly defines, **Flux dispatchers** dispatches the actions to the subsequent stores. Dispatchers can be called as a registry of callbacks. All the stores are registered with the dispatchers.

Some key points of dispatcher are the following:

* There is only one dispatcher per app.
* Dispatchers being used as a center for all the registered callbacks.
* It functions as a broadcaster of all the actions to the stores. Dispatchers acts as a queue, which sequentially broadcasts the actions. This is different from generic pub-sub systems in the following two ways:
    1. Callbacks are not subscribed to particular events. Every payload is dispatched to every registered callback.
    2. Callbacks can be deferred in whole or part until other callbacks have been executed.

- The dispatcher has the capability to invoke the callbacks in the order specified, and it waits for other updates (`waitFor()` method does that).

- In the flux library (`npm install flux`) node_module, the `register()` and `dispatch()` methods are defined, in the flux `library_app`, within the dispatcher class.

See the file located at `library_app/node_modules/Flux/lib/Dispatcher.js`:

```
// Registers a callback to be invoked with every dispatched
payload. Returns
// a token that can be used with `waitFor()`.

Dispatcher.prototype.register = function register(callback) {
  var id = _prefix + this._lastID++;
  this._callbacks[id] = callback;
  return id;
};
```

Thus, when the dispatchers receive the trigger (actions) from the Actions, it dispatches all the actions to the registered stores, one by one. This dispatching-flow is initiated with the `dispatch()` method, which passes the payload (data) to the registered store and has the callback registered to it.

The following code is an excerpt from the `Flux.js` library within the node_modules for the dispatcher:

```
/**
 * Dispatches a payload to all registered callbacks. The highlighted
code below ensures the fact that dispatches cannot be triggered in the
middle of another dispatch.

 */

Dispatcher.prototype.dispatch = function dispatch(payload) {
  !!this._isDispatching ? process.env.NODE_ENV !== 'production'
  ? invariant(false, 'Dispatch.dispatch(...):
  Cannot dispatch in
  the middle of a dispatch.') : invariant(false) : undefined;
  this._startDispatching(payload);
  try {
    for (var id in this._callbacks) {
      if (this._isPending[id]) {
        continue;
      }
      this._invokeCallback(id);
    }
```

```
    } finally {
      this._stopDispatching();
    }
  };
```

Let's create `AppDispatcher` for our `BookStore` app now.

The file `app-dispatcher.js` file should be created under the dispatcher directory of the `src`.

 AppDispatcher is an instance of the dispatcher from the Flux package with some additional properties (action in this case).

It has the `handleViewAction` method, which passes the action to be passed to the registered store via the callback.

The following is the code snippet from our app specific `app-dispatcher` class.

The file location is at `library_app/src/js/dispatchers/app-dispatchers.js`:

```
var Dispatcher = require('flux').Dispatcher;
var assign = require('react/lib/Object.assign');

var AppDispatcher = assign(new Dispatcher(),{
      handleViewAction: function(action){
        console.log('action',action);
        this.dispatch ({
          source: 'VIEW_ACTION',
          action: action
        })
      }
});

module.exports = AppDispatcher;
```

Before implementing the `library_app` store, let's check whether our payload (data) is printing out in the console. In order to do so, a handler function is created in the React `component` `app.js`, which is called when any part of the heading **My First Flux App** is clicked.

The file location is `library_app/src/js/components/app.js`:

```
var React = require('react');
var ReactDOM = require('react-dom');

//call the AppActions directly, before creation of the Store
var AppActions = require('../actions/app-actions');

//create a App component
```

```
var App = React.createClass({
      handler: function(){
        AppActions.addBook('This is the book..Sherlock Holmes')
      },
      render:function(){
        return <h1 onClick={this.handler}>My First Flux App </h1>
      }

});
module.exports = App;
```

> Run the httpster from your application's root directory:
>
> **doel@doel-Vostro:~/reactjs/ch6_flux_library$httpster**
>
> **Starting HTTPster v1.0.1 on port3333 from /home/doel/ reactjs/ch6_flux_library**

Open the browser and check the console, after clicking on the heading:

A screenshot from library_app

For a quick recap about the flow of our bookstore app till now:

The default `index.html` page serves the static content (Sample Application) on `localhost:3333`

The `index.html` page internally calls the `main.js`, which internally creates the React class and renders the content in the `<App />` React component (from the `src/js/components/app.js`). The React component is rendered in the `div` tag with ID `main`

Once we click on any portion of the `<App />` component (**My First Flux App**), an `onClick` event handler triggers the `handler()` function, which calls, `AppActions.addBook(This is the book..Sherlock Holmes)`, here, `AppActions` in the `AppConstant.AddBook` is the specific action to be called with the `payload` / `item`/ `data` (`This is the book..Sherlock Holmes`).

Once `AppActions.addBook` method is called, it is assigned to the callback `handleViewAction` of the dispatcher, with the following:

- `actionType: AppConstants.ADD_BOOK`
- ` item:` `This is the book..Sherlock Holmes`
- The `handleViewAction` method of the dispatcher passes the action (with `action_type` and `item`) and logs the output in the console and dispatches it.
- We see the following output in the `console.log` after clicking on **My First Flux App**:

  ```
  action Object { actionType: "ADD_BOOK", item: "This is the
  book..Sherlock Holmes" }
  ```

- This is just a way to pass the JS objects (`item: "This is the book..` `Sherlock Holmes"`) in a uniform and expected manner for the store to handle. It simplifies the data flow of the application and makes tracing and debugging easier.

Stores

Flux stores can be comparable with the models in MVC, though essentially they are not the same. From similar point of view, they are the same as all the business logic and computations happen in the Flux store. According to the Facebook team, "Stores manage the state of many objects — they do not represent a single record of data like ORM models do. Nor they are the same as Backbone's collections. More than simply managing a collection of ORM-style objects, stores manages the application state for a particular **domain** within the application."

Source `https://en.wikipedia.org/wiki/Object-relational_mapping`.

> *Object Relational Mapping (ORM) in computer science is a programming technique for converting data between incompatible type systems in object-oriented programming languages. This creates, in effect, a "virtual object database" that can be used from within the programming language. In object-oriented programming, data management tasks act on object-oriented (OO) objects that are almost always nonscalar values. For example, consider an address book entry that represents a single person along with zero or more phone numbers and zero or more addresses. This could be modeled in an object-oriented implementation by "Person object" with attributes/fields to hold each data item that the entry comprises: the person's name, a list of phone numbers, and a list of addresses. The list of phone numbers would itself contain "PhoneNumber objects" and so on. The address book entry is treated as a single object by the programming language (it can be referenced by a single variable containing a pointer to the object, for instance). Various methods can be associated with the object, such as a method to return the preferred phone number, the home address, and so on.*

The store(s) receives the action(s) from the dispatchers. Depending on the registered callback (with the dispatcher), the Store decides whether it should respond to the action dispatched by the dispatcher. No objects outside the app are responsible for changing the values within the Store or the Views. Thus any change, which is brought by the actions, results in the data change based on the registered callbacks and never by any setter methods.

As the Flux stores update themselves without any external intervention, hence it reduces the complexities typically found in MVC applications. The Flux stores controls what happens within them, only the input is via the dispatchers. In a MVC app, interdependency of various models with various views may lead to instability and complicated test cases.

A single app can have multiple stores, based on its functionality, but each store deals with a single domain. A store exhibits characteristics of both collection of models and a singleton model of a logical domain.

The following is quick recap of Stores Functionality:

- Stores register itself with the dispatchers through callbacks.
- Computations of the business logic reside in the stores as JS functions.
- After the action been dispatched from the dispatcher to the Stores, they are identified by the registered callbacks.
- The action is acted upon within stores by the state update.

- JS arrays: `_library` and `_readingItems` store the books available and what the reader wants to read.

- `EventEmitter` is a class of the events module, which is part of the Node. js core library. In this example, the event emitter function is done by the `eventEmitter.on()` method, where the first argument is the event, and the second argument is the function to be added. Thus, the `eventEmitter.on()` method simply registers the function. When the the `emit()` method is called, then it executes all the functions that are registered with the on method.

- The public methods `getReadingList()` and `getLibrary()` allow us to get the computed data from the `_readingItems` and `_readingList` JS arrays.

- `dispatcherIndex` in the `app-stores.js` code is used in order to store the return value of the dispatcher's registration method.

- The switch statement is the determining factor, in case of a dispatcher's broadcast, for what actions has to be performed. If a relevant action is taken, a change event is emitted and views that are listening for this event update their states.

The following is the code for `app_stores.js` for our `library_app`. It has all the business logic and computations of our app:

```
var AppDispatcher = require('../dispatchers/app-dispatchers');
var AppConstants = require('../constants/app-constants');
var assign = require('react/lib/Object.assign');

//eventEmitter allows the Stores to listen/broadcast changes to the
//Controller-Views/React-Components
var EventEmitter = require('events').EventEmitter;

var CHANGE_EVENT = 'change';

var _library = [];

for(var i=1; i<6; i++){
  _library.push({
    'id': 'Book_' + i,
    'title':'Sherlock Holmes Story ' + i,
    'description': 'Sherlock Series by Sir Arthur Conan Doyle'
  });
}

var _readingItems = [];
```

```
function _removeItem(index){
  _readingItems[index].inReadingList = false;
  _readingItems.splice(index, 1);
}

function _increaseItem(index){
  _readingItems[index].qty++;
}

function _decreaseItem(index){
  if(_readingItems[index].qty>1){
    _readingItems[index].qty--;
  }
  else {
    _removeItem(index);
  }
}

function _addItem(item){
  if(!item.inReadingList){
    item['qty'] = 1;
    item['inReadingList'] = true;
    _readingItems.push(item);
  }
  else {
    _readingItems.forEach(function(cartItem, i){
      if(cartItem.id===item.id){
        _increaseItem(i);
      }
    });
  }
}
var AppStore = assign(EventEmitter.prototype, {
  emitChange: function(){
    this.emit(CHANGE_EVENT)
  },
  addChangeListener: function(callback){
    this.on(CHANGE_EVENT, callback)
  },
  removeChangeListener: function(callback){
    this.removeListener(CHANGE_EVENT, callback)
  },
  getReadingList: function(){
    return _readingItems
```

```
  },
  getLibrary: function(){
    return _library
  }
```

 dispatcherIndex is used to store the return value of the Dispatchers registration method. dispatcherIndex is used in case of waitFor() method, that is when one part of the app has to wait for another part of the app to get updated.

The following is the code that shows the dispatcherIndex:

```
dispatcherIndex: AppDispatcher.register(function(payload){
    var action = payload.action;
    switch(action.actionType){
      case AppConstants.ADD_BOOK:
        _addItem(payload.action.item);
        break;

      case AppConstants.DELETE_BOOK:
        _removeItem(payload.action.index);
        break;

      case AppConstants.INC_BOOK_COUNT:
        _increaseItem(payload.action.index);
        break;

      case AppConstants.DEC_BOOK:
        _decreaseItem(payload.action.index);
        break;
    }

    AppStore.emitChange();

    return true;
  })
})
module.exports = AppStore;
```

Controller-Views and Views

Views are primarily the React Views, which essentially generate the actions. Controller-View listens to our stores, for any `changeEvent` been broadcasted. The `emitChange` events let our Controller-Views know if any change has to be performed into the state of the view or not. They are essentially React components. In our code, we have five such react components, as follows:

- `app-addbooktoreadinglist.js`
- `app-booklist.js`
- `app.js`
- `app-readinglist.js`
- `app-removefromreadinglist.js`

The following is the code for `app-booklist.js`:

```
var React = require('react');
var AppStore = require('../stores/app-stores');
var AddBookToReadingList = require('./app-addbooktoreadinglist')

function getLibrary(){
  return {items: AppStore.getLibrary()}
}

var BookList = React.createClass({
  getInitialState:function(){
    return getLibrary()
  },
  render:function(){
    var items = this.state.items.map(function(item){
      return (
        <tr key={item.id}>
          <td>{item.title}</td>
          <td><AddBookToReadingList item={item} /></td>
        </tr>
      );
    })
    return (
      <table className="table table-hover">
        {items}
      </table>
    )
  }
});

module.exports = BookList;
```

The following is the code that is internally called on the `AddBookToReadingList` React component:

```
var React = require('react');
var AppActions = require('../actions/app-actions');

//create a AddBookToLibrary component
var AddBookToReadingList = React.createClass({
        handleClick: function(){
            AppActions.addBook(this.props.item)
        },
        render:function(){
            return <button onClick={this.handleClick}>I want to borrow
</button>
        }

});
module.exports = AddBookToReadingList;
```

At the end, the following component `<Booklist \>` is added in the `app.js`. This is essentially for the part where a user can see the books they have in the `ReadingList` list section:

```
var React = require('react');
var AppStore = require('../stores/app-stores.js');
var RemoveFromReadingList = require('./app-
removefromreadinglist');

function readingItems(){
   return {items: AppStore.getReadingList()}
}

var ReadingList = React.createClass({
  getInitialState:function(){
    return readingItems()
  },
  componentWillMount:function(){
    AppStore.addChangeListener(this._onChange)
  },
  _onChange: function(){
    this.setState(readingItems())
  },
  render:function(){
    var total = 0;
    var items = this.state.items.map(function(item, i){
```

```
    return (
        <tr key={i}>
          <td><RemoveFromReadingList index={i} /></td>
          <td>{item.title}</td>
          <td>{item.qty}</td>
        </tr>
    );
  })
  return (
    <table className="table table-hover">
        <thead>
            <tr>
              <th></th>
              <th>Book Name</th>
              <th>Qty</th>
              <th></th>
            </tr>
        </thead>
        <tbody>
        </table>
  )
 }
});
module.exports = ReadingList
```

Revisiting the code

In each of the React components (readingList and bookList), getInitialState()
is initialized with the store public method getReadingList() and getLibrary(),
respectively.

Various methods are executed at precise points in a component's lifecycle.

- componentWillMount() is a React lifecycle method. It is invoked once, both
  on the client and server, immediately before the initial rendering occurs. If
  you call setState within this method, render() will see the updated state
  and will be executed only once despite change in the state:

```
componentWillMount:function(){
   AppStore.addChangeListener(this._onChange)
},
_onChange: function(){
   this.setState(readingItems())
}
```

- Thus, `componentWillMount()` is listening to the `addChangeListener` (defined in the `AppStore` store). If the `_onChange` parameter is passed, then the current object (`_this`) is updated (`setState`) with the new/updated data/payload (`readingItems`).

- In order to remove the items from the reading list, the event listener (`handleClick`) is unmounted.

The following is the code of app-`removebookfromreadinglist.js`:

```
var React = require('react');
var AppActions = require('../actions/app-actions');

//create a DeleteBookFromLibrary component
var DeleteBookFromReadingList = React.createClass({
        handleClicr: function(){
          AppActions.deleteBook(this.props.index)
        },
        render:function(){
          return <button onClick={this.handleClicr}>Book
          Completed</button>
        }
});
module.exports = DeleteBookFromReadingList;
```

The following is the code of `app.js`:

```
var React = require('react');
var BookList = require('./app-booklist');
var ReadingList = require('./app-readinglist');
//create a App component
var App = React.createClass({
        render:function(){
            return <div><h1>Book List</h1><BookList /><h1>Reading List</
h1><ReadingList /></div>
        }
});
module.exports = App
```

The final view of our `library_app` Flux application

On clicking on the button **I want to borrow**, the corresponding book will come to my Reading List. Once I am done with the book, click on the button **Book Completed**, to remove the book from the reading list.

The following is a screenshot of our `library_app` application.

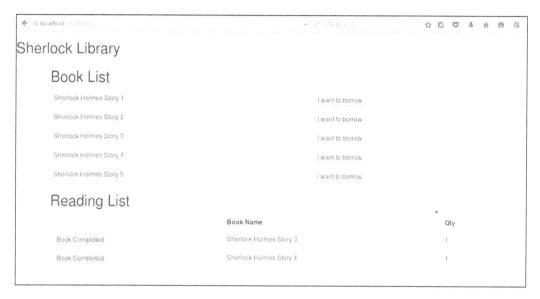

How to run this Flux app will be covered in the building and deployment structure later.

The following are the details of the components of a Flux-based app:

- Actions
- Dispatchers (registry of callbacks)
- Stores (callbacks registered with dispatchers)

- Views
- Controllers Views

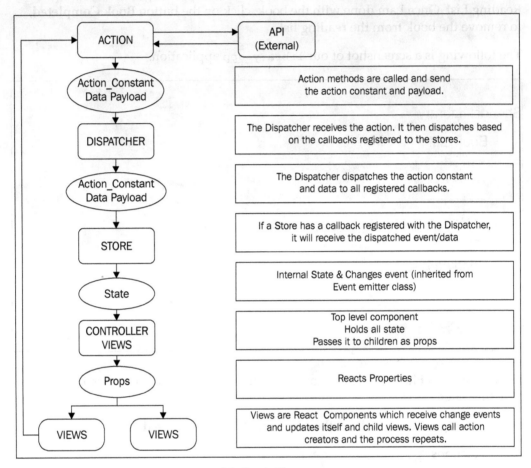

data flow in Flux app

Summary

Through our `libary_app` application, we have explored how the unidirectional data flow in a simple Flux-based application. The users can see the booklist in the views. They can add books in the reading list, thus the actions (adding books) gets passed to the dispatchers. Internally the dispatchers have the registered callbacks with the stores. The stores then adds/removes the books based on the user's action and computes the business logic and re-renders the changes accordingly again to the views.

In the next chapter, we will cover React good practices and patterns. This includes practices to develop reusable components, how to structure your components hierarchically to a better data flow, and how to validate your components behavior. In our app, we'll be improving our components developed so far.

7
Making Your Component Reusable

Until now, we have dug into React's components' lifecycle, properties, state, and ECMAScript with respect to React 0.1.13 and future versions. In this chapter, we will also see how we can write reusable components/code in React applications. Such reusable components in React are named Mixins. Furthermore, we will explore how the React component's properties can be validated.

The following topics to be covered in this chapter:

- Understanding mixins
- A higher order component in ECMA6 (as Mixin is not supported in ECMA6)
- Different types of validations in a React application
- The structure of a React component and application's architecture

Understanding Mixins

The Mixins (reusable components) are typically those React components that are used in multiple places and thus can be reused. Typically, the design elements, such as buttons, layout components, form fields, or any code logic/computation, that are used more than once are extracted in code named Mixin. Thus, Mixins help us incorporate some additional functionalities to existing React components by acting as helpers.

 Like in the previous chapters , the index.html content remains the same. Only the contents of the corresponding js (having the React components) changes.

Exploring Mixins by example

In this example we are setting the interval of the window global objects for every 100 ms:

Content of index.html:

```
<!DOCTYPE html>
            <html>
<head>
<script src="https://cdnjs.cloudflare.com/ajax/libs/react/0.14.0-rc1/
react.min.js"></script>
<script src="https://cdnjs.cloudflare.com/ajax/libs/react/0.13.3/
JSXTransformer.js"></script>
  <script src="https://cdnjs.cloudflare.com/ajax/libs/react/0.14.0-
rc1/react-dom.js"></script>

<meta charset="utf-8">
  <title>JS Bin</title>
</head>
<body>
  <div id="myReactContainer">
        <script type="text/jsx", src="index.js"></script>
  </div>
</body>
</html>
```

Content of index.js:

```
//Defining the Mixin
 . var ReactMixin = {
 . getInitialState:function(){
 .     return {count:0};
 .  },

// componentWillMount, a  lifecycle method, is added as a part of the
Mixin.
 . componentWillMount:function(){
    console.log('Component will mount!');
  },
  increaseCountBy10: function(){
    this.setState({count: this.state.count+10})
 }
  }
```

```
//This method displays text to display
    var App = React.createClass({
  render:function(){
   return (
     <div>
     <Label txt="SetInterval increase by 10 in every 100ms" />
       </div>
     )
  }
  });
```

```
// React component (<Label />), called from the <App /> component.
  var Label = React.createClass({
```

```
// Mixins are called using the keyword Mixin, followed by the Mixin
name within an array.
  mixins:[ReactMixin],
  componentWillMount:function(){
```

```
    //setting the interval to 100ms
      interval = setInterval(this.increaseCountBy10,100);
  },
```

```
//The function is called for the second time to update the interval
every 100ms
  componentWillUnMount:function(){
  clearInterval(this.interval);
  },
  render:function(){
   return <label>{this.props.txt} : {this.state.count}</label>
  }
 });
```

```
ReactDOM.render(<App />,
document.getElementById('myReactContainer'));
```

Run the httpserver from the application's root dir:

doel@doel-Vostro-3500:~/reactjs/ch7_mixins_
validationProps/app1_mixin$ httpster

Starting HTTPster v1.0.1 on port 3333 from /home/doel/
reactjs/ch7_mixins_validationProps/app1_mixin

The following is the output for this code on opening `localhost:3333`:

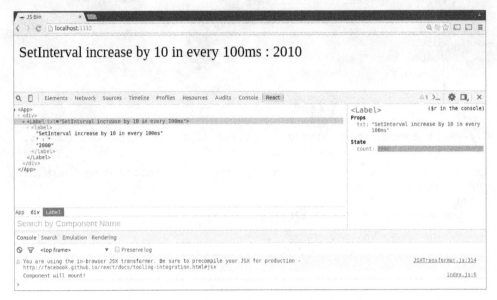

The app screenshot using Mixin with a lifecycle method

The explanation of the executed code:

A mixin is nothing but a JavaScript object, which can be reused within the React component later. We begin with defining the Mixin.

The `componentWillMount` is a lifecycle method, which is added as a part of the Mixin. Later, when the Mixin is called from the react component, the log from `console.log` can be seen in the bottom part of the developer tool portion of the webpage to present **Component Will Mount**.

We add a typical react component (`<App />`), which calls the `<Label />` component. It's a render function, which displays the text presented on the label. The App component can have multiple react components, which will internally call different react components.

In the next example, we will see such an example.

React component (`<Label />`) is called from the `<App />` component. It's using the React Mixin (ReactMixin).

In line mixins:[ReactMixin], Mixins in React, are called using the keyword Mixin, followed by the Mixin name (ReactMixin in this case), within an array. We can define multiple Mixins, as JavaScript objects. All these separate Mixins can then be called from a single React component (each Mixin representing a separate element in an array).

We will explore such an example, with multiple Mixins, later in the chapter.

We then add the `setInterval()` function

- The `setInterval()` method is a window function in JavaScript.
- It's declared as `window.setInterval(function, milliseconds)`.
- Although it's a method based on window object, but it's not necessary to call the `setInterval()` method on the window object, such as in the previously mentioned code. It can be called without the window prefix.
- The first parameter is the function that gets executed (`this.increaseCountBy10`).
- The second parameter is the interval of time between executions of each of the function, `this.increaseCountBy10`. The interval is set to `100ms` in this case.

The lifecycle method (`componentWillMount`) is then called for the second time in the previously mentioned code. For the first time, it is called within the Mixin body, which logs the `Component Will Mount` on the log.

For the second time, it is called within the React component (`<Label />`). Due to the second call, the `setInterval()` method is incrementing the value from `0` (count set to `0` initially) to `10`, in each `100` ms.

Take a look at the Facebook documentation `https://facebook.github.io/react/docs/reusable-components.html`:

"A nice feature of Mixins is that if a component is using multiple Mixins and several Mixins define the same lifecycle method (i.e. several Mixins want to do some clean up when the component is destroyed), all of the lifecycle methods are guaranteed to be called. Methods defined on Mixins run in the order Mixins were listed, followed by a method call on the component."

We will see another example of Mixins in the next section:

```
Calling Multiple Mixins from a single React Component
```

We shall now see another example where multiple Mixin will be called from a single React component. The following code is declared:

First, we shall declare two react Mixins:

```
var ReactMixin1= {

    getDefaultProps: function () {

        return {text1: "I am from first Mixin"};

    }

};

var ReactMixin2 = {

    getDefaultProps: function () {

        return {text2: "I am from second Mixin"};

    }

};
```

In the Second part of the code, we will call both the React Mixins, from the react component <App />:

```
var App = React.createClass({

  Mixins:[ReactMixin, ReactMixin2],

  render: function () {

    return (

    <div>

        <p>Mixin1: {this.props.text1} </p>

        <p>Mixin2: {this.props.text2}</p>

    </div>

    );
```

```
    }
  });
```

```
  ReactDOM.render(<App />,
  document.getElementById('myReactContainer'));
  \\
```

Execute the command httpster from application root directly like before to see the output from two Mixins:

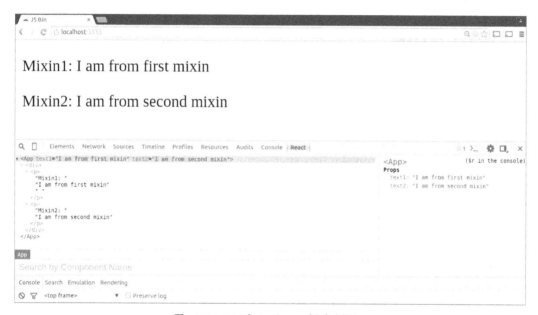

The app screenshot using multiple Mixins

Note the following:

- The same property name in both the Mixins, for example, *text*, in this case, will throw an error

- The same method name within the different Mixins will throw an error

- The same lifecycle methods can be called both within Mixin and within a React component. The order of execution of these lifecycle methods is Mixin, followed by a React component.

- In case the same lifecycle method is called within different Mixins, then the order of execution is in the order in which the Mixins are called within the array [lower to higher index].

Higher-order components in Mixins

In ReactJS using ES6, Mixins are no longer supported. Instead of this, they have introduced higher order components.

These higher order components are widely used in the Relay framework, which is a complete React-based framework released by Facebook. The higher order component wraps up child UI components. Thus, these components when called will first execute its queries and thereby render the child UI component(s). When the query is passed, data is passed from the child component to the higher order component in as props.

Validations

Validations are an integral part of any application dealing with user input. In ReactJS, there are some validations provided by the library that enables the developer to validate the data received.

Data are received mostly as properties (props) in react application. The various validators are exported from `React.PropTypes`. Any validation error, if occurs, will appear in the JavaScript console. Any such error occurring due to validation check will only occur in the development mode due to performance reasons.

Take a look at the Facebook ReactJS development team documentation `https://facebook.github.io/react/docs/reusable-components.html#prop-validation`. The following is an example of the various validators:

```
React.createClass({
  propTypes: {
    // You can declare that a prop is a specific JS primitive. By
    default, these
    // are all optional.
    optionalArray: React.PropTypes.array,
    optionalBool: React.PropTypes.bool,
    optionalFunc: React.PropTypes.func,
    optionalNumber: React.PropTypes.number,
    optionalObject: React.PropTypes.object,
    optionalString: React.PropTypes.string,

    // Anything that can be rendered: numbers, strings, elements
    or an array
    // (or fragment) containing these types.
    optionalNode: React.PropTypes.node,
```

```
// A React element.
optionalElement: React.PropTypes.element,

// You can also declare that a prop is an instance of a class.
This uses
// JS's instanceof operator.
optionalMessage: React.PropTypes.instanceOf(Message),

// You can ensure that your prop is limited to specific values
by treating
// it as an enum.
optionalEnum: React.PropTypes.oneOf(['News', 'Photos']),

// An object that could be one of many types
optionalUnion: React.PropTypes.oneOfType([
  React.PropTypes.string,
  React.PropTypes.number,
  React.PropTypes.instanceOf(Message)
]),

// An array of a certain type
optionalArrayOf:
React.PropTypes.arrayOf(React.PropTypes.number),

// An object with property values of a certain type
optionalObjectOf:
React.PropTypes.objectOf(React.PropTypes.number),

// An object taking on a particular shape
optionalObjectWithShape: React.PropTypes.shape({
  color: React.PropTypes.string,
  fontSize: React.PropTypes.number
}),

// You can chain any of the above with `isRequired` to make
sure a warning
// is shown if the prop isn't provided.
requiredFunc: React.PropTypes.func.isRequired,

// A value of any data type
requiredAny: React.PropTypes.any.isRequired,
```

```
    // You can also specify a custom validator. It should return
    an Error
    // object if the validation fails. Don't `console.warn` or
    throw, as this
    // won't work inside `oneOfType`.
    customProp: function(props, propName, componentName) {
      if (!/matchme/.test(props[propName])) {
        return new Error('Validation failed!');
      }
    }
  },
  /* ... */
});
```

An example using the isRequired validator

The index.html page. Use different JS pages in order to check the different versions of the validations used:

```
<!DOCTYPE html>
<html>
<head>
<script src="https://cdnjs.cloudflare.com/ajax/libs/react/0.14.0-rc1/
react.js"></script>
<script
src="https://cdnjs.cloudflare.com/ajax/libs/react/0.13.3/JSXTransf
ormer.js"></script>
  <script
  src="https://cdnjs.cloudflare.com/ajax/libs/react/0.14.0-
  rc1/react-dom.js"></script>
  <script type="text/jsx", src="index4.js"></script>

<meta charset="utf-8">
  <title>JS Bin</title>
</head>
<body>
  <div id="myReactContainer">
        <script type="text/jsx", src="index.js"></script>
  </div>
</body>
</html>
```

As the name of the validation suggests, the `isRequired` validator ensures that the property of the React component remains present. Otherwise, it will throw an error in the JS console. The `React.PropTypes.{foo}` properties are the JavaScript functions, which internally check whether a prop is valid or not. When the prop is valid, it will return `null`, but when the prop is invalid, then it returns an error. In *Chapter 4, Stateful Components and Events* we dug into ES6. In the next example, we will be using the ES6 syntax:

```
"use strict"

class App extends React.Component {

  render () {

    return (

      <div className="app">

        <h1 ref="title" className="app__title"></h1>

        <div ref="content"
        className="widget__content">{this.props.content}</div>

      </div>

    )

  }

}



App.propTypes = {

  title: React.PropTypes.string.isRequired,

  content: React.PropTypes.node.isRequired

}



ReactDOM.render(<App content="I am learning
react"/>,document.getElementById('myReactContainer'));
```

Run the httpster from your app's root dir in order to see the output in your browser's localhost:3333

The output will be as shown here:

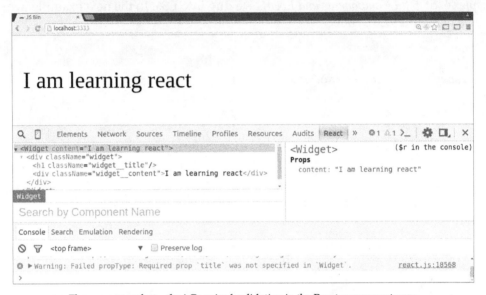

The app screenshot—the isRequired validation in the React component prop

A few points from the ES6 point of view with respect to the previously mentioned code:

use strict has been used opt in to a restricted variant of JavaScript. This is used as we are using let instead of var. use strict allows to place a component in a strict operating context and prevents certain actions from being taken and throws more exceptions.

let declares variables that are limited in scope to the block, statement, or expression on which it is used.

See the details at https://developer.mozilla.org/en-US/docs/Web/JavaScript/Reference/.

An example using custom validator

The following is the template, generally used while using custom validation in the code:

```
error = propTypes[propName](props, propName, componentName, location);
```

Let's go through an example of our own with custom error messages and use a few of these validations and see how it validates in the JavaScript console:

```
var ValidationApp = React.createClass({

   propTypes: {

      name: function(props, propName,componentName){

         if(!(propName in props))   {

            throw new Error("Property Name Missing ")

         }
      },

   render:function(){
      return <h1>{this.props.name}</h1>
   }
});
 ReactDOM.render(<ValidationApp />,
document.getElementById('myReactContainer')); //missing prop name
```

 Run the httpster from your app's root dir in order to see the output in your browser's `localhost:3333`

The output of this code is shown in this screenshot:

The app screenshot—custom validation in the React component prop

We can add more validations in the property (name) as:

```
var ValidationApp = React.createClass({

  propTypes: {

    name: function(props, propName,componentName){

      if(!(propName in props))  {

        throw new Error("Property Name Missing ")

      }



      if(props[propName].length < 7) {

        throw new Error("Can you add a longer Property Name, more than
7chars")

      }


    }

  },

  render:function(){

    return <h1>{this.props.name}</h1>

  }

});



// ReactDOM.render(<ValidationApp />, document.getElementById('myReact
Container')); //missing prop name

ReactDOM.render(<ValidationApp name="react" />,
document.getElementById('myReactContainer')); //prop length
should be more than 7 chars
```

Run the httpster from your app's root dir in order to see the output in your browser's `localhost:3333`

The output of the following code is shown here:

The app screenshot — validation in React component prop

Thus, if we pass the name property with more than seven chars, there would be no error in the JS console, as expected.

The structure of component

Now that we have explored quite a lot regarding ReactJS, there might be queries in your mind about how to architecture a react component or more broadly a react application as a whole. There are no ground rules that have been set, which is ideal while writing an application based on ReactJS. However, if we dig into the tutorials by the Facebook documentation team, hyperlink `https://facebook.github.io/react/docs/tutorial.html`, we will be able to understand the underlying way they have used while writing such an app.

Let's explore first how a component is structured mostly:

1. The component `declaredData` is fetched from the server [if required].

2. The `propTypes` of the component are declared [used for validations].

3. Component lifecycle methods [`componentWillMount`, `componentDidMount`, `componentDidUpdate`, `componentWillUnmount`, and so on] are defined.

4. Within each of these lifecycle methods, the functions of these methods are either declared or called internally from another JS functions, defined explicitly for a particular task. It's to be remembered that the previously mentioned lifecycle methods are not necessary to use all at the same time/ any in an application.

5. The render method, which has to be present within any react component. Thus, the way to structure any react-based application varies application-wise. Although there is no best way, but like any other application, it's advisable to compartmentalize the code in order to follow separation of concerns. We should separate the react views, components and data. One component directory can call other child component(s) as and when required, which thereby increases readability and testability of the code.

React being an open source JavaScript library, there are various open source sites and developers who are working on this library each day in order to enhance and tweak the library, as required.

For an application, using the ReactJS library, typically the views (React views) are separated as per their function (for example, home page, admin page, and product catalog). With each of the subfolder within the view, you can add the test.js file or you can keep all the test-related files under the same tests folder. In case you need some react views, which should be shared across other components, you can keep all those related files under the shared/lib folder.

Summary

In this chapter, we explored how we can develop reusable components in ReactJS (Mixins, before ES6 implementation). We also came to know about the higher order components, which are used later in the latter versions of ReactJS (from 0.13), which support ES6 and doesn't support Mixins. Validations are an integral part of any application, especially those using user input (that is, form inputs). We explored how ReactJS deals with validations and how we can use our custom validations as well. We got an overview how the react components are structured. In the following chapter, we will be dealing with the testing, in a React application.

8
Testing React Components

Until now, we have explored React's components lifecycle, properties, state, validations, and ECMAScript with respect to React 0.1.13 and future versions. In this chapter, we will explore the testing of JavaScript and ReactJS-related stuffs. First, we will be going through the testing as a whole using different JavaScript test frameworks and how we can run the tests, followed by testing views build with the ReactJS library.

The following are the things we will be covering in this chapter:

- Testing in JavaScript using Chai and Mocha
- ReactTestUtils to test React components
- Exploring Jest
- Testing React-based app using Expect, Mocha, and Shallow rendering

There are various ways that you can mix and match while testing JavaScript. Let's have a brief overview of the various things such as frameworks, assertion libraries, and testing tools. The list given here is not an exhaustive one, and covering all of them in detail is beyond the scope of this book.

Mocha and **Jasmine** are testing frameworks. They can be used with various testing assertion libraries as follows:

- `should.js` which is an assertion library. It is framework agnostic and works from IE9 and higher. The details of the library can be found from `https://www.npmjs.com/package/should`.
- `chaijs` is also an assertion library, where we add plugins. It also works with the testing framework(s). The details of the library can be found online from `http://chaijs.com/karma`. It is a JavaScript testing tool, which enables to test JavaScript codes in browsers. It's framework agnostic (can be used to run Mocha, Jasmine, Qunit, and so on). The details can be found at `https://www.npmjs.com/package/karma`.

It should be remembered that karma is neither a JavaScript framework like Jasmine or Mocha nor an assertion library like `chaijs` or `should.js`. This, we should use the assertion library and the framework as required along with karma in order to launch the HTTP server so that we can test the JS code in browsers.

Jest is also a framework on Jasmine framework. The Facebook developer team suggests the use of Jest for testing React-based applications. According to the Jest website (`https://facebook.github.io/jest/`), these are some advantages of using Jest instead of vanilla jasmine for testing purposes:

- Jest provides multiple layers on top of Jasmine
- It automatically searches and finds tests for you to execute
- It mocks dependencies for you while you run the tests
- It runs tests in parallel, hence finishing executing them faster
- It allows you to test asynchronous code synchronously
- It enables you to run tests on the command line with the fake DOM implementation via jsdom

Testing in JavaScript using Chai and Mocha

As discussed earlier, in order to write test cases for the React code, we will be installing some testing libraries to run tests and write assertions. Let's walk through the setup for the Chai assertion library and the Mocha testing framework. We need to install the libraries with the help of npm.

In the terminal type:

```
npm i -D mocha chai
```

install shortform: i

devDependencies shortform: D (the package will be installed only in a development environment)

After the Chai and Mocha libraries are installed by the previously mentioned command, they can be found under the `node_modules` directory.

We need to add the Mocha and Chai entries in our `package.json` file.

Package.json code

```
{
  "name": "JSApp",
  "version": "1.0.0",
  "description": "Get random numbers",
  "main": "index.js",
  "scripts": {
    "test": "mocha test.js"
  },
  "devDependencies": {
    "chai": "3.2.0",
    "mocha": "2.2.5"
  }
}
```

According to `https://docs.nodejitsu.com/articles/getting-started/npm/what-is-the-file-package-json`

All `npm` packages contain a file named `package.json`. This file is usually found in the project root. This file holds all metadata relevant to the project. A `package.json` file is used to offer information to `npm` thus allowing it to identify the project as well as handle the project's dependencies efficiently.

- `name`: This depicts the name of the application.

- `version`: This is a version of the application.

- `description`: This is general description of the application.

- `main`: This is the main JavaScript file, which may internally call other JS files. In this example, it's `index.js` file.

- `scripts`: This is the script to be executed when we call `npm` start. It should execute the test (mocha `test.js` file).

- `devDependencies`: These are the packages that are installed in the same directory as in `package.json`, unless the `-production` flag is passed on it. The packages are not installed on any other directory unless the `-dev` option is passed.

Add a `test.js` file. In order to check the setup working properly, we are adding a simple single test assertion.

Test.js file code

```js
var expect = require('chai').expect
, name = 'my Name';

var random = require('./index');

describe('random', function() {
  it('should work!', function() {
    expect(false).to.be.false;
  });

  it ('return my Name', function() {
        expect(name).to.be.a('string');
        expect(name).to.equal('my Name');
        expect(name).to.have.length(7);
        })
});
```

 `assertions` are called from Chai.

`describe` is called from Mocha framework to describe the tests.

Now we run the test, from the app's root directory in terminal, as shown here:

`npm test`

```
> JSApp@1.0.0 test /home/doel/reactjs/testing_jest_ch8/app2_mocha_chai
> mocha src/index.test.js



random
  ✓ should work!
  ✓ return my Name


2 passing (17ms)
```

A console screenshot using the Mocha and Chai setup

Testing using ReactTestUtils

ReactTestUtils is used to test React-based components. It can simulate all the JavaScript-based events, which ReactJS supports. The documentation is cited in the Facebook developer site (`https://facebook.github.io/react/docs/test-utils.html`).

The code is as shown for the stimulate function:

```
Simulate.{eventName}(
  DOMElement element,
  [object eventData]
)
```

Installing React and JSX

As mentioned earlier, while installing the Chai and mocha, we are here installing React- and JSX-specific test tools (ReactTestUtils) in order to ease our task. Let's explore the ReactTestUtils with help from some React-based components and stimulate them to test the behavior and functionality.

The following is an example of such a code.

We need to install the `jest` package via `npm` with the following code in the terminal:

```
sudo npm install jest-cli -save-dev
```

sudo/root access to the machine/server where the node packages has to be installed is required. This is particularly required as the directory where the node is installed. We can check the installed directory, using the following command:

```
npm config get prefix
```

As per the screenshot here, it's installed in the /usr directory, which has the permissions set to root. Hence, we need to install the npm packages using the sudo option.

```
doel@doel-Vostro-3500:~/reactjs/flux-library-ch6/node_modules/flux/dist$  npm config get prefix
/usr
doel@doel-Vostro-3500:~/reactjs/flux-library-ch6/node_modules/flux/dist$ ll /usr/
total 172
drwxr-xr-x  11 root root  4096 Oct  7 21:11 ./
drwxr-xr-x  25 root root  4096 Feb  2 11:24 ../
drwxr-xr-x   2 doel doel 61440 Feb 17 10:42 bin/
drwxr-xr-x   2 root root  4096 Oct  7 21:11 etc/
drwxr-xr-x   2 root root  4096 Sep 14 14:06 games/
drwxr-xr-x  54 root root 20480 Feb 17 10:40 include/
drwxr-xr-x 174 root root 36864 Feb 17 10:40 lib/
drwxr-xr-x  11 root root  4096 Jul 27  2015 local/
drwxr-xr-x   2 root root 12288 Feb 17 10:41 sbin/
drwxr-xr-x 314 root root 12288 Feb  2 23:10 share/
drwxr-xr-x  34 root root  4096 Feb  2 11:23 src/
```

A console screenshot of the /usr directory file owner/permissions.

Another way is to set the permission of the /usr directory to the user, which can have permissions to own and modify the files in the directory:

```
sudo chown -R $(whoami) $(npm config get
prefix)/{lib/node_modules,bin,share}
```

Let's try to have a approach of **test-driven development** (TDD) , whereby we will be creating a failing test case following the actual code to pass.

Create a JS file, which will greet any name with hi:

```
// greeting.js

module.exports = greetings;
```

Now, let's create the test file within a directory named __test__:

```
// __tests__/greeting-test.js

jest.dontMock('../greetings');

//executed when the test runs
describe('greetings', function() {
  it('greets the name', function() {
  var greet = require('../greetings');
  expect(greet("react")).toBe("hi react");
  });
  });
```

Let's recap about some jest properties, from the earlier-mentioned code:

- `jest.dontMock` is explicitly mentioned here, as jest by default mocks everything. Thus in order to test the actual code without mocking we need to ask jest not to mock the code which has to be tested (`greetings.js`)

- `describe('greetings', function())` each describe block is the test suite which gets executed when the test runs (`npm test/jest`). One describe block can have multiple test cases.

- `it('greets the name', function()`, it block the actual test spec/case within the describe block.

In order to execute the tests within the `__test__/` directory, we need to have the `package.json` file with the following entries:

 We will be covering more about packaging in the next chapter.

Here is the code for `package.json` file:

```
{
  "dependencies": {
    "react": "~0.14.0",
    "react-dom": "~0.14.0"
  },
  "devDependencies": {
    "jest-cli": "^0.8.2",
    "react-addons-test-utils": "~0.14.0"
  },
  "scripts": {
    "test": "jest"
  },
  "jest": {
    "unmockedModulePathPatterns": [
      "<rootDir>/node_modules/react",
      "<rootDir>/node_modules/react-dom",
      "<rootDir>/node_modules/react-addons-test-utils",
      "<rootDir>/node_modules/fbjs"
    ]
  }
}
```

Let's have a quick recap of the this code within `package.json`.

Once all are ready, we can run the test in the terminal, using the following command:

npm test

The output is shown as here:

```
> @ test /home/doel/reactjs/testing_jest_ch8/jest1
> jest

Using Jest CLI v0.8.2, jasmine1
 FAIL  __tests__/greetings-test.js (0.024s)
●greetings › it greets the name
  - ReferenceError: greetings is not defined
        at Object.eval (greetings.js:5:18)
        at Spec.eval (__tests__/greetings-test.js:6:16)
1 test failed, 0 tests passed (1 total in 1 test suite, run time 1.168s)
npm ERR! Test failed.  See above for more details.
```

The TDD console screenshot, showing failing tests.

Now, let's add the code so that the name is greeted with the name and the test passes:

```
// greeting.js

function greetings(name) {
   return "hi "+name;
}
module.exports = greetings;
```

Now, when we execute the test, we will be seeing a passing test case:

```
doel@doel-Vostro-3500:~/reactjs/testing_jest_ch8/jest1$ npm test

> @ test /home/doel/reactjs/testing_jest_ch8/jest1
> jest

Using Jest CLI v0.8.2, jasmine1
 PASS  __tests__/greetings-test.js (0.03s)
1 test passed (1 total in 1 test suite, run time 1.967s)
```

The TDD console screenshot, using npm test, showing passing tests.

One of the other ways to execute the tests is by installing `jest` and executing them by calling the jest from the terminal:

sudo npm install -g jest-cli

The output is as shown here:

```
doel@doel-Vostro-3500:~/reactjs/testing_jest_ch8/jest1$ jest
Using Jest CLI v0.8.2, jasmine1
 PASS  __tests__/greetings-test.js (0.047s)
1 test passed (1 total in 1 test suite, run time 1.712s)
```

The TDD console screenshot, using jest, showing passing tests.

Thus, we can see with either of the commands `npm test`/`jest`, we are getting the same output.

The jestTypical example of a Testsuite with Mocha, expect, ReactTestUtils and Babel

Let's see a typical example of `package.json`, which is using the following:

- Mocha as a testing framework
- Expect as an assertion library
- ReactTestUtils to test react-based JavaScript components
- Babel used as a transcompiler, which changes the ES6 codes into currently compatible (ES5) JavaScript code.

The example of `package.json` file:

```
"scripts": {
    "test": "mocha './src/**/*.test.js' --compilers js:babel-core/
register",
  },
  "devDependencies": {
    "babel-core": "6.1.4",
    "babel-loader": "6.1.0",
    "babel-preset-es2015": "6.1.4",
    "babel-preset-react": "6.1.4",
    "babel-preset-stage-2": "6.1.2",
    "mocha": "2.3.3",
    "react-addons-test-utils": "0.14.3",
  }
}
```

As in the previous examples, within the script object, we keep the the test files and all the test files follow the convention of ending with the `.test.js` extension. Any extension for the test files can be used. For compilation from ES6 code to browser compatible JS code, the `-compiler` tag is added in the script.

Install all the following packages, as here, mentioned in `package.json`:

```
npm install babel-loader babel-preset-es2015 babel-preset-react babel-
preset-stage-2 react-addons-test-utils
Babel being the transpiler, we need to add the following entry to enable
the import (reserver keyword) in the following .babelrc file:
```

```
{
    "presets": ["es2015"]
}
```

Here is the definition of a transpiler. Source `https://en.wikipedia.org/wiki/Source-to-source_compiler`

> *"A source-to-source compiler, transcompiler, or transpiler is a type of compiler that takes the source code of a program written in one programming language as its input and produces the equivalent source code in another programming language."*

The `.babelrc` file contains all the Babel API options. The following is the screenshot of the file structures of the app with test suite setup. The details can be found in the Babel documentation at https://babeljs.io/docs/usage/babelrc/.

```
doel@doel-Vostro-3500:~/reactjs/testing_jest_ch8/app4_withBabel$ ll
total 28
drwxrwxr-x  4 doel doel 4096 Jan  1 23:32 ./
drwxrwxrwx  9 doel doel 4096 Jan  1 22:12 ▮/
-rw-rw-r--  1 doel doel   30 Jan  1 23:23 .babelrc
-rwxrwxrwx  1 doel doel   93 Jan  1 03:14 greetings.js*
drwxr-xr-x 15 doel doel 4096 Jan  1 23:32 node_modules/
-rwxrwxrwx  1 doel doel  540 Jan  1 22:57 package.json*
drwxrwxr-x  2 doel doel 4096 Jan  1 23:51 __test__/
```

The screenshot showing the dir structure of a typical JS Application with the __test__ , node_modules, package.json, and .babelrc

Using the same `greetings.js` file as before but testing with the new ES6 syntax in the `greetings.test.js` and `index.test.js` files, let's test the testsuite.

Code __test__/greetings.test.js (using ES6 syntax)

```
import expect from 'expect';
describe('greetings', () => {
```

```
    it('greets the name', () => {
      var greet = require('../greetings');
      expect(greet("react")).toBe("hi react");
    });
  });
```

Code __test__/index.test.js (using ES6 syntax)

```
import expect from 'expect';
  describe('setup',() => {
    it('testing the setup is working', () => {
      expect(true).toEqual(true);
    });
      });
```

```
doel@doel-Vostro-3500:~/reactjs/testing_jest_ch8/app4_withBabel$ npm test

> @ test /home/doel/reactjs/testing_jest_ch8/app4_withBabel
> mocha './__test__/*.test.js' --compilers js:babel-core/register


greetings
  ✓ greets the name

setup
  ✓ testing the setup is working

2 passing (17ms)
```

A screenshot showing tests using ES6 syntaxes, mocha, and babel

Executing this test file using ES6 syntaxes with the mocha testing framework, expect assertion library and after been transpiled by Babel yielded the same result as before.

Testing with shallow rendering

Shallow rendering is a method used while testing React components in which the component is "one level deep". Such a shallow-rendered test component has the facts regarding the returned things with respect to the `render` methods. Such components do not have the child components attached to it, and it does not require DOM.

Thus, while testing with a shallow rendering method, it should be remembered that any changes in the parent component that has the DOM changes and/or any child components been changed may require in rewriting the test.

Let's explore this with help of some code. In the following example, we will be creating a React component (GreetingComponent) where the render method will return a div with two children (h2 and span elements).

The code of greeting.js:

```
// greeting.js

import React from 'react';

const { div, h2, span} = React.DOM;



export default React.createClass({

  displayName: 'GreetingComponent',

  render(){

    return (

    div({classname: 'Greeting'},

      h2({classname: "heading2"}, "Hi"),

      span({classname: "like"},"ReactJs")

    )

    );

  }

});
```

Let's write the test for this React code using the shallow rendering method.

Code of __test__/greeting.test.js

```
// Importing the necessary libraries and JavaScript code to be tested
import expect from 'expect';
import React from 'react';
import TestUtils from 'react-addons-test-utils';
import GreetingComponent from '../greetings.js';
```

```
describe('GreetingComponent', () => {
  it('should greet with the name', () => {

  // Creating a shallow rendered object and stored within  renderer
      const renderer = TestUtils.createRenderer();

  /*creating the react element (GreetingComponent, declared in the
  greeting.js code). This might be comparable to the "place" where the
  component to be tested is rendered. This component can respond to
  events and update itself
  */
      renderer.render(React.createElement(GreetingComponent));
  /* method is called on the renderer (TestUtils.createRenderer()) and
  stored within output. We can inspect this output in the console */
      const output = renderer.getRenderOutput();
      console.log(output);
      expect(output.type).toBe('div');
```

The output value is printed in the console. Based on that, we can see the different hierarchy and values of the concerned react component. The following is output from console.log (output)

```
GreetingComponent
[ '$$typeof': Symbol(react.element),
  type: 'div',
  key: null,
  ref: null,
  props: { classname: 'Greeting', children: [ [Object], [Object] ] },
  _owner: null,
  _store: {} }
```

The screenshot showing the renderedOutput() method in the console.

Let's go a level deep and check the value of the following: const output = renderer.getRenderOutput().props.children.

Thus, we can see the exact two children with their types and values of the GreetingComponent React `div` element:

```
GreetingComponent
[ { '$$typeof': Symbol(react.element),
    type: 'h2',
    key: null,
    ref: null,
    props: { classname: 'heading2', children: 'Hi' },
    _owner: null,
    _store: {} },
  { '$$typeof': Symbol(react.element),
    type: 'span',
    key: null,
    ref: null,
    props: { classname: 'like', children: 'ReactJS' },
    _owner: null,
    _store: {} } ]
```

The screenshot showing the renderedOutput() method of the children in the console.

Based on the output, we can test both the children (h2 and span) of the `div` element of the React GreetingComponent as follows:

Code of __test__/greeting.test.js

```javascript
import React from 'react';
import TestUtils from 'react-addons-test-utils';
import GreetingComponent from '../greetings.js';

describe('GreetingComponent', () => {

  it('should greet with the greeting Hi', () => {

    const renderer = TestUtils.createRenderer();
    renderer.render(React.createElement(GreetingComponent));
    const output = renderer.getRenderOutput();
    console.log(output);
    expect(output.type).toBe('div');

    expect(output.props.children[0].type).toBe('h2');
    expect(output.props.children[0].props.classname).toBe('heading2');
    expect(output.props.children[0].props.children).toBe('Hi');

  });
```

```
it('should return the like as ReactJs', () => {

    const renderer = TestUtils.createRenderer();

    renderer.render(React.createElement(GreetingComponent));

    const output = renderer.getRenderOutput();

    console.log(output);

    expect(output.type).toBe('div');

    expect(output.props.children[1].type).toBe('span');

    expect(output.props.children[1].props.classname).toBe('like');

    expect(output.props.children[1].props.children).toBe('ReactJs');

});


});
```

We can see that there are several lines of codes that are common between the two `it` blocks. Hence, we can separate these common codes and refactor it as shown here:

```
// __tests__/sum-test.js

//jest.dontMock('../greetings.js');

import expect from 'expect';
import React from 'react';
import TestUtils from 'react-addons-test-utils';
import GreetingComponent from '../greetings.js';

describe('GreetingComponent', () => {
  describe('Common code', () => {
    const renderer = TestUtils.createRenderer();
    renderer.render(React.createElement(GreetingComponent));
    const output = renderer.getRenderOutput();
//    console.log(renderer);
    console.log("From Common Code");
```

```
            console.log(output);


        it('should greet with the greeting Hi', () => {
    //       console.log(renderer);
            console.log("h2 component");
            console.log(output);
            expect(output.props.children[0].type).toBe('h2');
        expect(output.props.children[0].props.classname).toBe('heading2');
            expect(output.props.children[0].props.children).toBe('Hi');
        });

        it('should return the like as ReactJs', () => {
    //       console.log(renderer);
            console.log("span component");
            console.log(output);

            expect(output.props.children[1].type).toBe('span');

            expect(output.props.children[1].props.classname).toBe('like');

            expect(output.props.children[1].props.children).toBe('ReactJs');

        });




    });

    });
```

While executing the code, we can get the output in a file, with the following command:

```
npm test > test_output.txt
```

The following is the output in the `test_output.txt` file. You can play and check the different properties of the React elements. The explanation of each of them is beyond the scope of this book. But we can see that all React components are nothing but JavaScript objects.

```
> @ test /home/doel/reactjs/testing_jest_ch8/app5_reactWithTesting
> mocha './__test__/*.test.js' --compilers js:babel-core/register

From Common Code
{ '$$typeof': Symbol(react.element),
  type: 'div',
  key: null,
  ref: null,
  props: { classname: 'Greeting', children: [ [Object], [Object] ] },
  _owner: null,
  _store: {} }


  GreetingComponent
    Common code
h2 component
{ '$$typeof': Symbol(react.element),
  type: 'div',
  key: null,
  ref: null,
  props: { classname: 'Greeting', children: [ [Object], [Object] ] },
  _owner: null,
  _store: {} }
^M      ✓ should greet with the greeting Hi
span component
{ '$$typeof': Symbol(react.element),
  type: 'div',
  key: null,
  ref: null,
  props: { classname: 'Greeting', children: [ [Object], [Object] ] },
  _owner: null,
  _store: {} }
^M      ✓ should return the like as ReactJS

  setup
^M    ✓ testing the setup is working


  3 passing (20ms)
```

Summary

We saw how we can test the different components in a React-based application and JavaScript as whole. In order to test a JavaScript code, we used chai and expect as assertion libraries, jasmine and jest as testing frameworks. To test a React application, we used ReactTestUtils and shallow rendering. In the following chapter, you will be learning about the deployment process of a React application. We will be exploring more about `package.json`, which we touched on in this chapter.

9
Preparing Your Code for Deployment

Going through the ReactJS fundamentals and flux, we have almost approached the end of this book. After developing any application, we are left with the most crucial part of making the application available to the outside world, thus deploying your application. It's a good practice to keep the code in a source control repository such as GitHub or Bitbucket and to version control the code using Git. These help while working in a group and retrieval of any code as and when necessary. The explanation of how to set up the earlier-mentioned things is beyond the scope of this book, but there are a plenty of resources available for the same.

In this chapter, we will be exploring the following topics:

- An introduction to Webpack
- The ways of deploying a React application using Webpack and Gulp
- The configuration options used for browserify
- Installing a simple web server

An introduction to Webpack

Webpack is a module bundler, which is used to deploy JavaScript-based applications. It takes the input as modules with dependencies and then outputs these into static assets.

From the Webpack documentation site (`https://webpack.github.io/docs/what-is-webpack.html#how-is-webpack-different`), the following image explains the same.

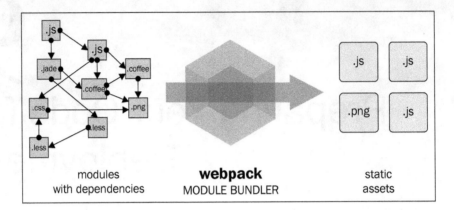

Building a simple React application

As in the earlier chapters, let's build a simple React-based application with which we will be integrating the Webpack and deploy thereafter.

Install the packages `vis` `npm` from a terminal as:

```
sudo npm install babel-loader babel-preset-es2015 babel-preset-react
babel-preset-stage-2
```

```
npm -g install httpster
```

httpster: It is a simple http server to run the static content. In chrome browser, the `index.html` file sometimes doesn't render due to the X-origin error. Hence, running this webserver from your application directory will be easier to test your application in Chrome. Just run the command `httpster`.

By default, the server runs in port `3333`, thus `localhost:3333` in the browsers should render the `index.html` page of your application.

We have created the following files:

- `src/bundle.js`: This is where Webpack writes its output to, after transpiling the code and performing any other transformations of the file to plain JS. The details of this file are discussed in the latter section.

- `index.html`: Application landing page.

- `index.js`: React-based components.

- `.babelrc`: presets and environments of babel are declared here.

- `node_modules`: Installed `npm` packages are present.

- `Webpack.config.js`: Webpack-related configurations are present here.

The following is a console screenshot, showing app directory structure using Webpack:

```
doel@doel-Vostro-3500:~/reactjs/app1$ sudo npm install -g webpack
[sudo] password for doel:
npm WARN optional dep failed, continuing fsevents@1.0.6
/usr/bin/webpack -> /usr/lib/node_modules/webpack/bin/webpack.js
webpack@1.12.10 /usr/lib/node_modules/webpack
├── interpret@0.6.6
├── tapable@0.1.10
├── clone@1.0.2
├── esprima@2.7.1
├── async@1.5.2
├── supports-color@3.1.2 (has-flag@1.0.0)
├── enhanced-resolve@0.9.1 (graceful-fs@4.1.2, memory-fs@0.2.0)
├── memory-fs@0.3.0 (errno@0.1.4, readable-stream@2.0.5)
├── optimist@0.6.1 (wordwrap@0.0.3, minimist@0.0.10)
├── mkdirp@0.5.1 (minimist@0.0.8)
├── webpack-core@0.6.8 (source-map@0.4.4, source-list-map@0.1.5)
├── loader-utils@0.2.12 (big.js@3.1.3, json5@0.4.0)
├── uglify-js@2.6.1 (async@0.2.10, uglify-to-browserify@1.0.2, source-map@0.5.3, yargs@3.10.0)
├── watchpack@0.2.9 (graceful-fs@4.1.2, async@0.9.2, chokidar@1.4.2)
└── node-libs-browser@0.5.3 (tty-browserify@0.0.0, https-browserify@0.0.0, path-browserify@0.0.0, constants-b
code@1.4.0, string_decoder@0.10.31, os-browserify@0.1.2, process@0.11.2, assert@1.3.0, domain-browser@1.1.7,
, timers-browserify@1.4.2, events@1.1.0, stream-browserify@1.0.0, vm-browserify@0.0.4, util@0.10.3, console-b
able-stream@1.1.13, url@0.10.3, http-browserify@1.7.0, buffer@3.6.0, browserify-zlib@0.1.4, crypto-browserify
```

Take a look at the simple React app code example:

index.html:

```
<!DOCTYPE html>
<html lang="en">
<head>
  <meta charset="UTF-8">
  <script
src="https://cdnjs.cloudflare.com/ajax/libs/react/0.14.0-
rc1/react.js"></script>
  <script src="https://cdnjs.cloudflare.com/ajax/libs/react/0.14.0-
rc1/react-dom.js"></script>
  <script
src="https://cdnjs.cloudflare.com/ajax/libs/react/0.13.3/JSXTransf
ormer.js"></script>
```

```
        <title>React App with Webpack</title>
    </head>
    <body>
      <div id="app"></div>
      <script type = "text/jsx" src="index.js"></script>
    </body>
    </html>
```

index.js:

```
"use strict";
class App extends React.Component {
  render() {
    return <div>Hello </div>;
  }


}
ReactDOM.render(<App />, document.getElementById('app'));

.babelrc:
{
  "presets": ["es2015",  "react"]
}
```

Setting up Webpack

Now that we got an overview of what Webpack is, let's install and configure it so that we can use it in our React application, as mentioned later.

In you terminal, type the following:

```
sudo npm install -g webpack
```

 The -g option installs the Webpack library globally in your computer.

As you can see, in the following screenshot, there are many dependent packages, which also gets installed while installing Webpack:

```
doel@doel-Vostro-3500:~/reactjs/app1$ ll
total 24
drwxrwxr-x  4 doel doel 4096 Jan  8 21:50 ./
drwxrwxrwx 17 doel doel 4096 Jan  8 17:40 ▮/
-rw-rw-r--  1 doel doel    0 Jan  8 21:48 bundle.js
-rw-rw-r--  1 doel doel    0 Jan  8 21:49 index.html
drwxrwxr-x  4 doel doel 4096 Jan  8 21:50 node_modules/
-rw-rw-r--  1 doel doel  221 Jan  8 17:45 package.json
drwxrwxr-x  2 doel doel 4096 Jan  8 20:12 src/
-rw-rw-r--  1 doel doel  327 Jan  8 20:13 webpack-config.js
```

A console screenshot, showing webpack package installation with all the dependencies

After Webpack's installation, we will be creating the `webpack-config.js` file, with entries given as follows:

```
// The declaration of the object having all the Webpack-related
configuration details.
module.exports = {

//entry point of the application
  entry: "./app/components/index.js",

/* In this bundle.js file,Webpack will have the output  after
transpilation of the code from index.js (ES6 to ES5) & combining
all the components' and it's children js files are present.
*/
  output: {
    filename: "src/bundle.js"
  },
  module: {
// Loading the test loader, it is used to transform any JSX code
in the tests into plain JavaScript code.

    loaders: [
      {
// All the packages which are installed within the node_modules
directories are to be excluded.
        test: /\.jsx?$/,
        exclude: /(node_modules)/,
```

```
//specifying which one to use
      loader: 'babel',
      query: {
        presets: ['react', 'es2015']
      }
    }
  ]
}
}
```

Let's explain the preceding code.

We start off with the entry point of our application. As React-based applications generally have many components, having a common entry point for all of these components will be easier to manage and important for well-structured modular applications.

We then direct the output to a file `bundle.js` and combine all components and its children.

After loading the test loader, we mention which packages are to be excluded within the `node_modules` directory.

We then use the loaders, specifying which one of them to use. The presets loader does all the transformations that Babel does while transpiling the ES6 code into the current browser-compatible code.

Let's run the Webpack command in our terminal now,

`sudo webpack -w -v`

- `sudo` is used as we need the sudo/root permission in order to execute the Webpack commands or we need to change the ownership/permissions of the specific directory.

  The `-w` option ensures to watch any file that changes. It'll watch the source files for changes, and when changes are made, the bundle will be recompiled. (Source: `https://webpack.github.io/docs/webpack-dev-server.html`).

  The `-v` option gives the verbose output.

- `webpack --help`: This command gives the output of all the options and their corresponding meanings, which can be passed as arguments.

```
doel@doel-Vostro-3500:~/reactjs/webpack_ch9/app1$ sudo webpack -w -v
Hash: 12a3374c336415079893
Version: webpack 1.12.10
Time: 8372ms
          Asset     Size  Chunks           Chunk Names
./src/bundle.js  1.76 kB       0  [emitted]  main
    + 1 hidden modules
Hash: bacafde43d68ac702113
Version: webpack 1.12.10
Time: 590ms
          Asset     Size  Chunks           Chunk Names
./src/bundle.js  3.62 kB       0  [emitted]  main
    + 1 hidden modules
```

A console screenshot, after the webpack execution on the terminal

Thus, all the transformations and transpirations of the code is there in the `src/bundle.js` output file.

Typical out of the `bundle.js` file from the app mentioned earlier:

```
/******/ (function(modules) { // webpackBootstrap

/******/     // The module cache

/******/         var installedModules = {};



/******/     // The require function

/******/     function __webpack_require__(moduleId) {



/******/         // Check if module is in cache

/******/         if(installedModules[moduleId])

/******/             return installedModules[moduleId].exports;
```

```
/******/            // Create a new module (and put it into the cache)

/******/            var module = installedModules[moduleId] = {

/******/                exports: {},

/******/                id: moduleId,

/******/                loaded: false

/******/            };



/******/            // Execute the module function

/******/            modules[moduleId].call(module.exports, module,
module.exports, __webpack_require__);

/******/            // Flag the module as loaded

/******/            module.loaded = true;



/******/            // Return the exports of the module

/******/            return module.exports;

/******/        }

/******/        // expose the modules object (__webpack_modules__)

/******/        __webpack_require__.m = modules;

/******/        // expose the module cache

/******/        __webpack_require__.c = installedModules;

/******/        // __webpack_public_path__

/******/        __webpack_require__.p = "";
```

```
/******/     // Load entry module and return exports

/******/     return __webpack_require__(0);

/******/ })

/**********************************************************************
****/

/******/ ([

/* 0 */

/***/ function(module, exports) {

    "use strict";

    var _createClass = function () { function
    defineProperties(target, props) { for (var i = 0; i <
    props.length; i++) { var descriptor = props[i];
    descriptor.enumerable = descriptor.enumerable || false;
    descriptor.configurable = true; if ("value" in descriptor)
    descriptor.writable = true; Object.defineProperty(target,
    descriptor.key, descriptor); } } return function (Constructor,
    protoProps, staticProps) { if (protoProps)
    defineProperties(Constructor.prototype, protoProps); if
    (staticProps) defineProperties(Constructor, staticProps);
    return Constructor; }; }();

    function _classCallCheck(instance, Constructor) { if
    (!(instance instanceof Constructor)) { throw new
    TypeError("Cannot call a class as a function"); } }

    function _possibleConstructorReturn(self, call) { if (!self) {
    throw new ReferenceError("this hasn't been initialised -
    super() hasn't been called"); } return call && (typeof call
    === "object" || typeof call === "function") ? call : self; }

    function _inherits(subClass, superClass) { if (typeof
    superClass !== "function" && superClass !== null) { throw new
    TypeError("Super expression must either be null or a function,
    not " + typeof superClass); } subClass.prototype =
    Object.create(superClass && superClass.prototype, {
    constructor: { value: subClass, enumerable: false, writable:
    true, configurable: true } }); if (superClass)
    Object.setPrototypeOf ? Object.setPrototypeOf(subClass,
    superClass) : subClass.__proto__ = superClass; }
```

```
     var App = function (_React$Component) {
        _inherits(App, _React$Component);

      function App() {
      _classCallCheck(this, App);

      return _possibleConstructorReturn(this,
      Object.getPrototypeOf(App).apply(this, arguments));
      }
    _createClass(App, [{
        key: "render",
        value: function render() {
            return React.createElement(
            "div",
            null,
            "Hello "
        );
        }
    }]);
    return App;
    }(React.Component);

    ReactDOM.render(React.createElement(App, null),
    document.getElementById('app'));
/***/ }
/******/ ]);
```

Refer to the Webpack documentation at `https://webpack.github.io/docs/`
`webpack-dev-server.html`.

The newly generated `bundle.js` is stored in the memory in a location, which is the
relative path specified in publicPath.

For example, with the preceding configuration, the bundle will be available at
`localhost:8080/assets/bundle.js`.

In order to load the bundled files, we create the html file (mostly named as the
`index.html` file) in the `build` folder from which static files are served:

```
<!DOCTYPE html>
<html lang="en">
<head>
```

```
  <meta charset="UTF-8">
  <title>Document</title>
</head>
<body>
  <script src="bundle.js"></script>
</body>
</html>
```

By default, the application runs in `localhost:8080/` to launch your app. For example, with the configuration mentioned earlier (with publicPath), go to `localhost:8080/assets/`.

Advantages of Webpack

Along the various advantages of using Webpack, as yet another bundler, these are the most important ones:

1. **Code splitting**: Based on the code size, it helps modularize the code chunks of code and loads these modules as and when needed. You can define the split points on your code, based on which the code chunks will be used. Thus, it helps in faster page load and performance improvement.

2. **Loaders**: As in the earlier-mentioned image, in the left-hand side, you can see that there are various other formats such as `coffescripts/jsx` instead of JavaScript and .less instead of `.css`. Thus, these loaders (`npm` packages) are used to convert these other formats into the accepted standardized formats, which makes the life of the developers much easy to code into any format they want. In React-based applications that we were seeing earlier, JSX formats are widely used. Hence, these loaders will come handy.

3. **Clever parsing**: It helps to parse most of the third-party library and handles the widely used styles in CommonJS and AMD.

4. **Plugin system**: In case you want to extend Webpack to create a step within the build process, you can create a plugin that uses a callback to the Webpack reference point, where you want to call it.

Introduction to Gulp

Now that we have seen a module bundler, let's see what Gulp will do for us. Gulp is a build tool for compiling and compressing JS/assets, and it does live reload on the browsers. Gulp file is basically a file with the set of instructions, which Gulp should do. The file can have a default task or several other tasks to be called from one another.

Installing Gulp and creating Gulp file

Let's install `gulp` and configure it with our existing application:

`npm install -g gulp (for globally installing gulp)`

`npm install gulp -save-dev (as a developer dependancy)`

Next, create a simple `gulpfile.js` file at the root of your app directory:

```
var gulp = require('gulp');

gulp.task('default', function() {
  // tasks goes here
});
```

Let's execute the command from terminal:

```
doel@doel-Vostro-3500:~/reactjs/webpack_ch9/app1$ gulp
[02:22:55] Using gulpfile ~/reactjs/webpack_ch9/app1/gulpfile.js
[02:22:55] Starting 'default'...
[02:22:55] Finished 'default' after 94 µs
```

A console screenshot, after the gulp command is executed

Then, we are installing some other packages for Gulp-related tasks. We are adding these in our `package.json` file and running `npm` install, in order to install these:

```
Package.json
{
  "name": "app1",
  "version": "1.0.0",
  "description": "ReactApp",
  "main": "index.js",
  "scripts": {
    "test": "echo \"Error: no test specified\" && exit 1"
  },
  "author": "Doel Sengupta",
  "license": "ISC",
  "dependencies": {
    "react": "^0.14.3",
    "react-dom": "^0.14.3"
  },
  "devDependencies": {
    "babel-core": "^6.3.13",
    "babel-loader": "^6.2.0",
```

```
    "babel-preset-es2015": "^6.3.13",
    "babel-preset-react": "^6.3.13",
    "browser-sync": "^2.9.6",
    "gulp": "^3.9.0",
    "gulp-babel": "^6.1.1",
    "gulp-concat": "^2.6.0",
    "gulp-eslint": "^1.1.1",
    "gulp-filter": "^3.0.1",
    "gulp-notify": "^2.2.0",
  }
}
```

A few of the key things in gulp:

- Initially, we need to require all the gulp and related gulp plugins/packages, which are required while executing the tasks

- The gulp tasks are declared with gulp.task.

- The .pipe command is used to stream data that needs to be processed. This command is used concatenated, which results in getting the output together.

Now if we add some tasks in the Gulp file, it will look like the following:

```
var gulp           = require('gulp');
var babel          = require('gulp-babel');
var browserSync    = require('browser-sync');
var concat         = require('gulp-concat');
var eslinting      = require('gulp-eslint');
var notify         = require('gulp-notify');
var reload         = browserSync.reload;

var jsFiles = {
  vendor: [

  ],
  source: [
    '*.js',
    '*.jsx',
  ]
};
```

```
// Lint JS/JSX files
gulp.task('eslinting', function() {
   return gulp.src(jsFiles.source)
     .pipe(eslinting({
        baseConfig: {
          "ecmaFeatures": {
             "jsx": true
          }
        }
     }))
     .pipe(eslinting.format())
     .pipe(eslinting.failAfterError());
});


// Watch JS/JSX  files
gulp.task('watch', function() {
   gulp.watch('*.{js,jsx,html}').on("change",reload);
});

// BrowserSync
gulp.task('browsersync', function() {
   browserSync({
     server: {
       baseDir: './'
     },
     open: false,
     online: false,
     notify: false,
   });
});
gulp.task('default', ['eslinting', 'browsersync', 'watch']);
```

Let's go through the preceding code:

- Four Gulp tasks are declared earlier and are highlighted. The **default** mandatory task is calling three tasks internally, as in the last highlighted line. In Gulp terms, any task calling other tasks are mentioned as array elements of the parent task.

- `gulp.task ('eslinting', function)`: This task is used to check any issue with the code in the `js` & `jsx` files. In order to check the `jsx` with `gulp-eslint` plugin, the `ecmaFeature: {"jsx": true}` option is set.

- `gulp.watch`: As the name suggests, this task watches any change in the JS files, and recompiles the files thereafter. In case it's not required to watch any files, we need to pass `read: false` to the `options` object. After the change in the `js/jsx` files, we can call `browserSync.reload` or add tasks in order to reload your html page.

- `browsersync`: This plugin is not officially for gulp; though it can work with any gulp task. Any change in the `js/jsx` files will be synced to the browser.

After executing the gulp command from app's root directory in the terminal, we should be able to see such an output in the terminal. See the following image:

```
doel@doel-Vostro-3500:~/reactjs/webpack_ch9/app1$ gulp
[00:06:16] Using gulpfile ~/reactjs/webpack_ch9/app1/gulpfile.js
[00:06:16] Starting 'eslinting'...
[00:06:16] Starting 'browsersync'...
[00:06:16] Finished 'browsersync' after 45 ms
[00:06:16] Starting 'watch'...
[00:06:16] Finished 'watch' after 18 ms
[BS] Access URLs:

 Local: http://localhost:3000

    UI: http://localhost:3001

[BS] Serving files from: ./
[00:06:17] Finished 'eslinting' after 341 ms
[00:06:17] Starting 'default'...
[00:06:17] Finished 'default' after 14 µs
[BS] Reloading Browsers...
[BS] Reloading Browsers...
```

A console screenshot, after the gulp command with tasks been executed

Let's check once how the `gulp-eslint` works. Add a line such as require 'react', at the beginning of the `index.js` file.

```
require "react";
var ReactApp1 = React.createClass({
  render: function(){
    return (
      <div>
        Hello World
      </div>
    )
  }
});
```

```
ReactDOM.render(<ReactApp1 />, document.getElementById('app'));
```

```
index.js
  1:10  error  Parsing error: Unexpected string

✖ 1 problem (1 error, 0 warnings)

[00:12:40] 'eslinting' errored after 333 ms
[00:12:40] ESLintError in plugin 'gulp-eslint'
Message:
    Failed with 1 error
```

A console screenshot, after the gulp command with an eslint task with error been executed

As we know, it should be `var React = require("react");` is the correct way of requiring the React package.

There are many for Gulp plugins, which are helpful in our day-to-day application development apart from the ones mentioned in the earlier-mentioned example. Please feel free to see the Gulp documentation and related plugins from their website `http://gulpjs.com/`.

Summary

In this chapter, we came to know how we can deploy our React applications using Webpack and the way Gulp eases our life by automating tasks, minifying our assets (JS, JSX, CSS, SASS, images, and so on), watching any changes on these files and live-reload built in the browser. In *Chapter 10, What's Next*, we will be exploring some advanced concepts of ReactJS.

10
What's Next

Until now, we have covered all the topics from building a React-based JavaScript application from scratch, integrating it with the Facebook Graph API, digging into the various stages of a component, it's life cycle, validating, testing, and deploying the apps. With that, we have reached the end of this book, but let's explore some advanced topics in React world.

In this chapter, we will be exploring the following topics briefly because it's not possible to cover everything in detail within one chapter:

- AJAX in React
- React Router
- Server-side rendering
- Isomorphic applications
- Hot reloading
- Redux React
- Relay and GraphQL
- React Native

AJAX in React

Like in any other applications, AJAX in a React-based application can be used to fetch data asynchronously. According to the Facebook documentation of loading the data from the server using AJAX (`https://facebook.github.io/react/tips/initial-ajax.html`), you need to remember some of the key points as mentioned here:

- Include the jQuery library in your HTML:

```
<script src="//code.jquery.com/jquery-1.12.0.min.js"></script>
```

Because there is no separate Ajax-only library from jQuery that can be used, the entire jQuery has to be used in a React-based application, while using Ajax. Downloading the minified version of jQuery from cdn results in much less load time.

Load the data in the life cycle phase of `componentDidMount`. This method occurs only once during the life cycle on the client, and any child components can be accessed in this phase. Any external js library or loading data using AJAX is advised to be done in this phase.

- The `isMounted` method is used to check whether the component is mounted in the DOM. Although this is used with AJAX before `setState()`, this method will be deprecated while using ES6 syntaxes, which use `React.component`, and may be entirely removed in future React versions. Refer to `https://facebook.github.io/react/docs/component-api.html`.

Here is the code of `index.html`:

```
<!DOCTYPE html>
<html>
<head>
<script src="https://cdnjs.cloudflare.com/ajax/libs/react/0.14.0-rc1/react.min.js"></script>
<script
src="https://cdnjs.cloudflare.com/ajax/libs/react/0.13.3/
JSXTransformer.js"></script>
  <script
  src="https://cdnjs.cloudflare.com/ajax/libs/react/0.14.0-rc1/react-
dom.js"></script>
<script src="//code.jquery.com/jquery-1.12.0.min.js"></script>
<meta charset="utf-8">
  <title>JS Bin</title>
</head>
<body>
  <div id="app">
        <script type="text/jsx", src="index.js"></script>
  </div>
</body>
</html>
```

The following is the code for `index.js`:

```
var GithubUser = React.createClass({
  getInitialState: function() {
    return {
      username: '',
      user_url: ''
    };
  },

  componentDidMount: function() {
    $.get(this.props.source, function(result) {
      console.log(result);
      var user = result;
      if (this.isMounted()) {
        this.setState({
          username: user.login,
          user_url: user.html_url
        });
      }
    }.bind(this));
  },

  render: function() {
    return (
      <div>
        {this.state.username}'s last gist is
        <a href={this.state.user_url}>here</a>.
      </div>
    );
  }
});
```

```
ReactDOM.render(
    <User source="https://api.github.com/users/doel" />,
    document.getElementById('app')
);
```

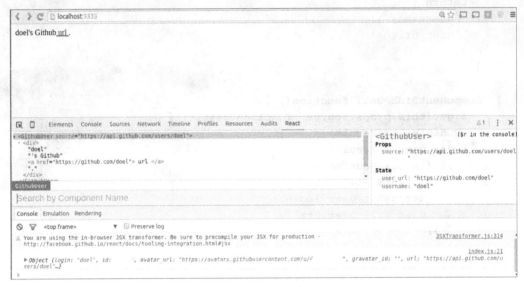

React with Ajax (`https://facebook.github.io/react/tips/initial-ajax.html`)

React Router

React Router is a library based on top of the React library, which helps in easy and quick routing of an application with multiple pages. Although it may be possible to build such a flow in the application without the React-router, as the application grows with many pages, it becomes cumbersome to identify the child-parent relationship between the pages. This is where React-router comes to our rescue, where it identifies how to build the nested UIs.

Sources:

- `https://github.com/reactjs/react-router`
- `https://www.npmjs.com/package/react-router`

Server-side rendering

Server-side rendering in ReactJS is done by JavaScript (NodeJS or io.js). This method actually prerenders the initial state of the React components at the server side. Thus, it is helpful in fast rendering of web pages, as the users can see the web pages without having to wait for the entire JavaScript at the client side to finish loading.

However, this kind of rendering should not be used for those applications where a huge amount of data has to be piped from the server to the client side, which may slow the page load. In such cases, we may use pagination or bulk load the data in chunks, which won't slow the page load, but can be fetched from the server side in specific time intervals.

The following two methods from the React API provides the backbone of server-side rendering (`https://facebook.github.io/react/docs/top-level-api.html`).

ReactDOMServer

The `react-dom/server` package allows you to render your components on the server.

The `ReactDOMServer.renderToString` method returns a string. It generates two additional DOM attributes — `data-React-id` and `data-React-checksum` — which are used internally by the ReactJS library.

This method renders an element of `ReactElement` to the initial HTML of the view and returns an HTML string.

It should only be used while using the server-side rendering and at the server side.

During the initial page load, sending this method from the server to the client results in faster page load and enables web crawling for **search engine optimization (SEO)**.

When the `ReactDOM.render()` is called to any node previously, React will attach event handlers on those nodes, resulting in faster page loads.

The syntax is:

```
string renderToString(ReactElement element)
```

The `ReactDOMServer.renderToStaticMarkup` method is similar to `renderToString`.

It is used mainly to generate static pages.

The syntax is:

```
string renderToStaticMarkup(ReactElement element)
```

In order to illustrate the example of the server-side rendering in ReactJS, we can use express (the minimalistic web framework for NodeJS applications) at the server side.

- The npm update
- The npm install express
- npm init: This will generate a package.json file

Add the content mentioned later in the index.js file to initiate a simple web application running on port 3000 using express. The same example can be found in the readme file of the node_modules/express directory:

```
var express = require('express');
//....Initialise the app variable requiring the express.
var app = express();

/* Denotes the basic routing by the express server.  */
app.get('/', function (request, response) {

  response.send('Hello World');

})

//  The following code will make the app listen in your localhost,
    i port 3000
app.listen(3000);
```

We first begin with declaring the app as an instance of express.

We then denote the basic routing by the express server. In this example, the express instance (app) is using the GET HTTP method. Thus, when app.get calls the default path (/) or any PATH on the server, the third parameter being the HANDLER, should send a response Hello World to the client (browser) when the route is matched.

The application runs on port 3000. You can run the app on any port as per your requirement.

Execute the application using the node command on the express file:

```
node index.js
```

Using express, we can now see the example of ReactJS server-side rendering:

- Within your app directory, execute the following command to download express:

```
npm install react express
```

- From the `express.js` file, we will be calling the React component

Here is the code for creating the `ReactComponent`, without using JSX:

The `ReactComponent.js` file:

```
var React = require('react')

var ReactComponent = React.createClass({

  render:function(){

    return React.createElement('li', null, this.props.argument)

  }

});

module.exports = ReactComponent;
```

After running the express with the above command as node index.js from your app's root dir in the terminal, we will be seeing the following screenshot in our browser's `localhost:3000`.

Express JS simple app

Here is the explanation on the earlier-mentioned code.

`createElement` is the primary type of React, which has four properties (`types`, `properties`, `keys`, `ref`). The highlighted code mentioned earlier means that it will create a React element of the type list (`li`), which does not have any property but will pass the values from the React-rendered component's property (whose key name is `argument`).

According to the Facebook documentation (`https://facebook.github.io/react/docs/top-level-api.html`) for the React API, the highlighted code with respect to `renderToStaticMarkup`

> string renderToStaticMarkup(ReactElement element),
>
> *"Similar to* renderToString, *except this doesn't create extra DOM attributes such as* data-react-id, *that React uses internally. This is useful if you want to use React as a simple static page generator, as stripping away the extra attributes can save lots of bytes."*

`renderToString` renders `ReactElement` to its initial HTML. This should only be used on the server. React will return an HTML string. You can use this method to generate HTML on the server and send the markup down on the initial request for faster page loads and to allow search engines to crawl your pages for SEO purposes.

If you call `ReactDOM.render()` on a node that already has this server-rendered markup, React will preserve it and only attach event handlers, allowing you to have a very fast first-load experience.

The code for the `express.js` file is:

```
var express = require('express');

var React = require('react');

var ReactComponent =
React.createFactory(require('./ReactComponent'));

var app = express();


function landingPage(request, response){

  var argument = request.params.argument || 'This is the default
  Landing Page in absence of any parameter in url';

  var reactComponent = ReactComponent({argument:argument});

  response.send(React.renderToStaticMarkup(reactComponent));

}
```

```
app.get('', landingPage);

app.get('/:argument', landingPage)

app.listen(4000)
```

After running the express with the above command as node index.js from your app's root dir in the terminal, we will be seeing the following screenshot in our browser's localhost:4000.

The screenshot of the application, React with server-side rendering, showing default pages. As we can see, the port in which the app is listening is 4000.

In case of dynamic routes, this is the screenshot of React with server-side rendering, showing other pages.

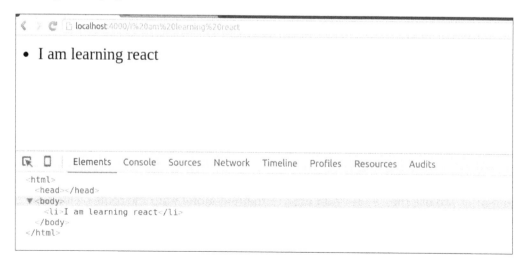

As mentioned earlier, if we use `renderToString` instead of `renderToStaticMarkup`, we can see two attributes such as `data-react-id` and `data-react-checksum` in the React component.

`data-react-id`: is the custom data attribute that the ReactJS library uses to specifically identify it's components within DOM. It can be present both at the client or the server side, whereas the one present at the server starts with a dot followed by some letters and then numbers, the IDs present at client side are only numbers.

The following example shows the earlier method `rederToString()`:

```
function landingPage(request, response){

    var argument = request.params.argument || 'This is the default
    Landing Page in absence of any parameter in url';

    var reactComponent = ReactComponent({argument:argument});

    response.send(React.renderToString(reactComponent));

}
```

Rerunning the express with the above changes, will render the following in the browser's `localhost:4000`, as depicted in the screenshot below.

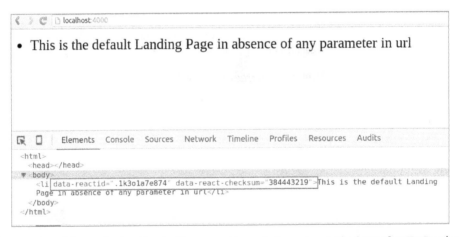

A screenshot of the application, React with server-side rendering, using method `renderToString`

To sum up, we can see that React-router is a library that is capable of running both at the server side and at the client side (browser). In order to use the server-side rendering, we use the `renderToString()` method along with the routes. During the request-response cycle, the React-router on the server matches with the requested route and renders the correct route from the server to the client (browser) using the `renderToString()` method of the React library.

Isomorphic applications

Isomorphic JavaScript applications are those where JavaScript is used both at the server and client side. Thus, the same React component can be used both at the client as well as at the server side. Some of the advantages of building such applications are:

- Whenever required, render the view at the server side based on the application state
    - The server will render the application in exactly the same way the client would have rendered for increased consistency

- In case the JavaScript in the browser is not working, the application would still work because the same JavaScript is present at the server side as well. You need to send the action to the server in order to attain the same result.

Hot reloading

Hot reloading is a term used in the JavaScript world, which is used to refer to live changes in the browser without the browser being refreshed. In the React ecosystem, React Hot Loader is widely used for the same purpose.

React Hot Loader is a plugin for Webpack, which results in instantaneous and live changes in the browser, without losing states. The changes can be visible while editing React components and functions as `LiveReload` for React.

Some limitations of the react hot loader first version have been discussed by the author (Dan Abramov) here at `https://medium.com/@dan_abramov/the-death-of-react-hot-loader-765fa791d7c4#.fc78lady9`. The details of the project can be found at `https://gaearon.github.io/react-hot-loader/`.

Redux React

Redux is a JavaScript library designed by Dan Abramov, which helps in containerization of the states for the JavaScript applications. As the application grows, the complexity rises due to the requirement of the back and forth state updatability between the model and the view. Redux came to the rescue to solve this crooked complex path of state mutation and asynchronism. Thus, it defines itself as an attempt to make predictable state mutations.

It can be used with React or any other view library. Some of the key points to be remembered while using Redux are as follows:

- The state of the JavaScript application is stored entirely inside the same object tree inside a *single store*. Thus, even when the application grows, it's easier to debug. The development phase is also faster as the entire application state is in one place. The state is read only; there are only getters in the state and no setters as you are unable to write to this store.

- Any change to the state can only be done by emitting an *action*. The action is nothing but an object that describes the changes that happened. These action objects can be logged, serialized, stored, and replayed later in order to debug. Except for these actions, no views or network callback can change the state. This restriction makes the changes in the state mutation predictable, without the hassle of looking out for any transient hidden changes.

- The third component in Redux is *reducers*. Reducers tell how the actions change the state tree. The reducers are nothing but functions that have the previous state and an action. The reducers therefore act as the setters for the state store as they are setting the new state. Any change to be performed is not on the actual state object but on the copy of the state object (new state object). A single root reducer can be used in simple applications, whereas you can delegate to multiple child reducers (by passing additional data) as the number of tasks grow.

Source:

- `http://redux.js.org/docs/basics/UsageWithReact.html`

Relay and GraphQL

Relay is a framework in ReactJS for **declarative data fetching**, which solves the problem of updating the data in a React-based application and where exactly it has to be updated. Using GraphQL, the Relay framework decouples *what* data is to be fetched from *how* it should be fetched.

GraphQL is like a query language to query a graph though not typically a graph like those represented in pie charts, x, y axes, or Venn diagrams.

- It's used to query from a relationship graph, where each node and the relationship between them are represented as edges.

- In order to fetch data from a subset of such a relationship-based graph, GraphQL is very useful.

- Unlike in representational state transfer (REST) where data is fetched from the server based on server endpoint using resources, in GraphQL data are fetched from the server based on the requirement by the client.

- Thus, the data is decoupled, and all the data are fetched at one go from the server within a single network request.

- Data can be stored and retrieved from a cache with ease and this results in faster performance.

- Any write operation is named a mutation. It's not a 1:1 relationship between the data change in the disk which GraphQL stores and returns to the developer. The best way is to use a query that is the intersection between the cached-date and the data that may change.

For an in-depth understanding of the Relay framework, refer to `https://facebook.github.io/relay/docs/thinking-in-relay.html#content`.

React Native

As the name suggests, **React Native** is used to build native applications in iOS and Android platforms using JavaScript and ReactJS. Some of the key features of React Native, favored by the Facebook developer teams (`https://facebook.github.io/react-native/`) for the native platforms, are mentioned here:

- It has the power of consistency in look and feel using React component counterparts

- You can develop the app using Chrome developer tools and run in a simulator

- There is asynchronous execution of all the code between the application and the native platform

- React Native seamlessly handles touch events, polyfills, StyleSheet abstraction, designing common UI layouts

- It's widely used to extend native code creating iOS and Android modules and views and reusing them later, with ease

- React Native's qualities of being declarative, asynchronous, and responsive are highly beneficial for iOS development

References

Note that the list here is nothing near to an exhaustive one, there are plethora of good articles, blog posts, and newer ones budding each new day.

Here are some of the sites to keep an eye on:

- `https://facebook.github.io/react/blog/`
- `https://egghead.io`
- `https://code-cartoons.com/`

The following are some of the communities on social media:

- `https://twitter.com/ReactJSNews`
- `https://twitter.com/reactjs`
- `https://twitter.com/dan_abramov`

Summary

ReactJS is a vibrant JS community. There are many changes and advancements in the JavaScript ecosystem happening on a daily basis. Keeping ourselves up to date is a mammoth and essential task. We can closely track the latest in JS world by following them on social platforms, question-answer forums, their websites, attending conferences and, last but not the least, always getting our hands dirty.

For any comments, suggestions or discussion feel free to contact us at `@ doelsengupta`, `@singhalmanu`.

Index

A

access token 41
actions
  defining 104, 105
AJAX, in React
  defining 173, 174
  references 174
  URL 173
API documentation
  URL 40
Atom
  about 6
  URL 6

B

Bower
  about 4
  ReactJS, installing with 5
  URL 5
Brackets
  about 6
  URL 6

C

CDN
  URL 46
chaijs
  about 139
  URL 139
code
  revisiting 117-120

communities, on social media
  references 186
component properties
  data flow, with properties 37-39
  defining 35, 36
component structure
  defining 137, 138
  URL 137
component style, JSX and Gotchas
  about 31
  CSS classes 32
  style 31
Content Distribution Network (CDN) 46
Controller-Views
  and Views 115, 116
CSS classes
  references 32

D

data centers
  URL 46
declarative data fetching 184
dispatchers
  defining 106-110
DOM (Document Object Model) 1

E

ECMAScript7
  URL 99
Emacs Editor
  URL 6

downloading 3, 4
files, serving through web server 10
installing, with Bower 5
installing, with NPM 4
maximum number of roots 21
properties, versus states 55
reference 10
references 2, 4
supported attributes 23
supported elements 24
URL 4
using 3
ReactJS component
data, rendering 50-54
ReactJS, with JSX
references 17
React Native
defining 185
URL 185
React Router
defining 176
ReactTestUtils
about 143
URL 143
used, for testing 143
React tools
URL 92
Redux React
defining 183, 184
Relay
about 184
and GraphQL 184, 185
Relay framework
references 185

S

search engine optimization (SEO) 177
server-side rendering
defining 176, 177
ReactDOMServer 177-182
URL 177
shallow rendering 149

should.js
about 139
URL 139
Single Page Application (SPA) 2
stateful component 56
stateless components 56
state property
defining 56
React state example,
        interactive form used 61-63
state, initializing 56, 57
state, replacing 59, 60
state, setting 57, 58
states 55, 56
stores
defining 110-114
functionality 111
Sublime Text
about 6
URL 6
supported attributes
URL 23
supported elements
HTML elements 24
references 24
SVG elements 25

T

test-driven development (TDD) **144**
testing
with shallow rendering 149-155
text editors 6
tools
about 5
Chrome Extension 7
text editors 6
used, for transforming JSX 18, 19
transpiler
reference 148
transpiling 92

V

validations
  defining 130
  example, custom validator used 134-137
  example, isRequired validator used 132-134
Views
  and Controller-Views 115, 116
Vim
  URL 6

W

Webpack
  about 157
  advantages 167
  setting up 160-167
  simple React application, building 158, 159
  URL 158
Webpack documentation
  URL 166